W9-CNW-103

Forest Brook H.S. Media Center

LITERATURE
and the GODS

$18.70

4/08/02 P.O.#83189

LITERATURE
and the GODS

Roberto Calasso

Translated
from the Italian
by Tim Parks

ALFRED A. KNOPF   NEW YORK   2001

This Is a Borzoi Book
Published by Alfred A. Knopf

Copyright © 2001 by Roberto Calasso
All rights reserved under International and
Pan-American Copyright Conventions. Published
in the United States by Alfred A. Knopf, a
division of Random House, Inc., New York, and
simultaneously in Canada by Random House
of Canada Limited, Toronto. Distributed by
Random House, Inc., New York.
www.aaknopf.com

Knopf, Borzoi Books, and the colophon are
registered trademarks of Random House, Inc.

Originally published in Italy as *La letteratura e gli
dèi* by Adelphi Edizioni, S.P.A., Milan. Copyright
© 2001 by Adelphi Edizioni S.P.A. Milano

ISBN: 0-375-41138-0

Manufactured in the United States of America
First American Edition

For Josephine

Contents

I

The Pagan School

The gods are fugitive guests of literature. They cross it with the trail of their names and are soon gone. Every time the writer sets down a word, he must fight to win them back. The mercurial quality that heralds their appearance is token also of their evanescence. It wasn't always thus. At least not so long as we had a liturgy. That weave of word and gesture, that aura of controlled destruction, that use of certain materials rather than others: this gratified the gods, so long as men chose to turn to them. After which, like wind-blown scraps in an abandoned encampment, all that was left were the stories that every ritual gesture implied. Uprooted from their soil and exposed, in the vibration of the word, to the harsh light of day, they frequently seemed idle and impudent. Everything ends up as history of literature.

So it would be a dull business indeed just to list the times the Greek gods turn up in modern poetry from the early Romantics on. Almost all the poets of the nineteenth century, from the most mediocre to the sublime, wrote a line or two in which the gods are mentioned. And the same is true of most of the poets of the twentieth century. Why? For all kinds of reasons: out of established scholastic habit—or to sound noble, or exotic, or pagan, or erotic, or erudite. Or—most frequently and tautologically—to sound poetic. But whether a poem chooses to name Apollo, or maybe an oak tree, or the ocean's foam, doesn't make much difference and can hardly be very meaningful: they are all terms from the literary lexicon, worn smooth by use.

Yet there was a time when the gods were not just a literary cliché, but an event, a sudden apparition, an encounter with bandits perhaps, or the sighting of a ship. And it didn't even have to be a vision of the whole. Ajax Oileus recognized Poseidon disguised as Calchas from his gait. He saw him walking from behind and knew it was Poseidon "from his feet, his legs."

Since for us everything begins with Homer, we can ask ourselves: which words did he use for such events? By the time the Trojan War broke out, the gods were already coming to earth less frequently than in an earlier age. Only a generation before, Zeus had fathered Sarpedon on a mortal woman. All the gods had turned up for the marriage of Peleus and Thetis. But now Zeus no longer showed himself to men; he sent other Olympians along to do his exploring for him: Hermes, Athena, Apollo. And it was getting harder to see them. Odysseus admits as much to Athena: "Arduous it is, oh goddess, to recognize you, even for one who knows much." The *Hymn to Demeter* offers the plainest comment: "Difficult are the gods for men to see." Every primordial age is one in which it is said that the gods have *almost* disappeared. Only to the select few, chosen by divine will, do they show themselves: "The gods do not appear to everyone in all their fullness [*enargeîs*]," the *Odyssey* tells us. *Enargés* is the *terminus technicus* for divine epiphany: an adjective that contains the dazzle of "white," *argós*, but which ultimately comes to designate a pure and unquestionable "conspicuousness." It's the kind of "conspicuousness" that will later be inherited by poetry, thus becoming perhaps the characteristic that distinguishes poetry from every other form.

But how does a god make himself manifest? In the Greek language the word *theós*, "god," has no vocative case, observed the illustrious linguist Jakob Wackernagel. *Theós* has a predicative function: it designates *something that happens*. There is a wonderful example of this in Euripides' *Helen*: "*O theoí. theòs gàr kaì tò gignóskein phílous*"—"O gods: recognizing the beloved is god." Kerényi thought that the distinguishing quality of the Greek world was this habit of "saying of an event: 'It is *theós*.'" And an event referred to as being *theós* could easily become Zeus, the most vast and all-inclusive of gods, the god who is the background noise of the divine. So when Aratus set out to describe the phenomena of the cosmos, he began his poem thus: "From Zeus let our beginning be, from he whom men never leave unnamed. Full of Zeus are the paths and the places where men meet, full of Zeus the sea and the seaports. Every one of us and in every way has need of Zeus. Indeed we are his offspring."

"Iovis omnia plena," Virgil would later write, and in these words we hear his assurance that this was a presence to be found everywhere in the world, in the multiplicity of its events, in the intertwining of its forms. And we also hear a great familiarity, almost a recklessness, in the way the divine is mentioned, as though to encounter divinity was hardly unusual, but rather something that could be expected, or provoked. The word *átheos*, on the other hand, was only rarely used to refer to those who didn't *believe* in the gods. More often it meant to be abandoned by the gods, meant that they had chosen to withdraw from all commerce with men. Aratus was writing in the third century B.C., but what became of this experience that for him was so obvious and all-pervasive in the centuries that followed? How did time affect it? Did it dissolve it, destroy it, alter and empty it beyond recognition? Or is it something that still reaches out to us, whole and unscathed? And if so, where, how?

One morning in 1851, Baudelaire tells us, Paris awoke with the feeling that "something important" had happened: something new, something "symptomatic," yet something that nevertheless presented itself as merely another *fait divers*. A word had been buzzing insistently in everybody's head: revolution. Now it so happened that, at a dinner party in honor of the revolution of February 1848, a young intellectual had proposed a toast to the god Pan. "But what has Pan got to do with the revolution?" Baudelaire asked the young intellectual. "Don't you know?" came the answer: "It's Pan who starts revolutions. He is the revolution." Baudelaire didn't leave it at that: "So it's not true that he's been dead for ages? I thought a loud voice had been heard drifting across the Mediterranean and that this mysterious voice that rang out from the Columns of Hercules as far as the shores of Asia had announced to the old world: THE GOD PAN IS DEAD." The young intellectual didn't seem worried. "It's just a rumor," he said. "Scandal mongers, nothing in it. No, the god Pan is not dead! The god Pan lives on," he insisted, lifting his eye to the heavens with quite bizarre tenderness: "He will return." Baudelaire glosses: "He was talking about the god Pan as if he were the prisoner of Saint Helena." But the exchange wasn't over; Baudelaire had another question: "So can we presume that you are pagan?" The young intellectual was positively disdainful: "Of course I am; don't you know that only paganism, if properly understood, that is, can save the world? We must go back to the true doctrines that were eclipsed, but *only for an instant*, by the infamous Galilean. And then, Juno has looked favorably on me, a look that went right to my soul. I was sad and miserable, watching the procession go by; I implored that beautiful divinity, my eyes were full of love, and she sent one of her looks, a profound and benevolent look, to cheer me up and give me courage." Baudelaire comments: "Juno threw him one of her *regards de vache, Bôôpis Éré*. Possibly the poor fellow is mad." This last joking remark is addressed to an anonymous third person, so far a silent observer, who now dismisses the affair thus: "Can't you see he's talking about the ceremony of the fatted calf? He was looking at all those rosy women with their *pagan* eyes, and Ernestine, who works at the Hippodrome and was playing Juno, tipped him an allusive wink, a really sluttish stare." By this time what had started out as the most magniloquent and visionary of exchanges has become pure Offenbach, an example of boulevardier wit that actually predates the boulevards themselves, albeit by very little. And the young intellectual winds up the conversation with the same ambiguous mix of registers: "Call her Ernestine all you like," said the young pagan. "You want to disappoint me. But the effect on my morale was the same—and think of that look as a good omen."

So with the *regard de vache* of a Juno of the Hippo-drome—which, as we remember, was a circus near the Arc de Triomphe that had burned down a few months previously—the gods of Olympus announced their return to the Parisian theatre circuit. And, as is so often the way in Paris, the Parisians announced as news—or at least as only really counting as news once it happened in Paris—something that actually had already manifested itself elsewhere and quite some time ago, in the Germany of Hölderlin and Novalis, for example, a good fifty years before: the reawakening and return of the gods. Yet Parisians had had the privilege of being introduced to that Germany by an illustrious explorer. When Madame de Staël began to travel the highways and byways of Germany like some journalist in search of the flavor of the day, the country was still very much the enchanted forest at the heart of Europe. No sooner were its leaves rustled than they stirred the chords of the Romantic piano. Madame de Staël didn't notice this, of course, her ears being attuned only to the ideas all around her—which she wielded like blunt instruments. Traveling beneath the huge open skies of a country where to her amazement she was seeing "traces of a nature uninhabited by man," her immediate response was one of discouragement: "Something oddly silent in both the landscape and its inhabitants saddens one at first."

Between the pert and ruthless chitter-chatter of Parisian society and this deep, brooding silence lay a distance more speculative than spatial. So the first odd thing this journalist observed was that on German soil "the empire of taste and the weapon of ridicule have no influence." Hence when the gods returned to manifest themselves here, they would not be immediately corroded by irony and sarcasm as in Paris. On the contrary, the danger here was that their appearance would be overwhelming. As indeed was the case for Hölderlin, dazzled by Apollo on his way home from Bordeaux: "As they tell of the heroes, I can say Apollo struck me down," he wrote to Böhlendorff. But in order for Apollo, "he who strikes from afar," to thrust himself with such violence on a German poet wandering through western France, "constantly moved by the celestial fire and the silence of men," and in order for "the celestial fire" actually to mean something frightening and enchanting again, rather than be just another ornamental flourish in a pompous *tragédie classique*, something had to happen that really was a "revolution," a powerful shaking of earth and sky. Which brings us back to the young Parisian intellectual whom Baudelaire obviously was mocking and who raised his glass to the god Pan, for the god Pan "is the revolution." And we note that Baudelaire wrote *L'École païenne* in 1852 while Hölderlin's letter to Böhlendorff is dated November 1802, exactly fifty years before. So what Baudelaire is talking about here was a case of involuntary parody, on the part of the young man, of an extreme experience—Hölderlin's in the period immediately preceding his madness. An experience that was quite unknown in France and hadn't even percolated through in Germany, if only because of the sacred terror it aroused. But events live on, have their meaning and do their work on their own, even when not immediately noticed. To understand how that incongruous toast to Pan could happen in Paris in 1851, one cannot avoid going back to Hölderlin on his way from Bordeaux. Fortunately there are some stepping stones in between. The first comes courtesy of Heinrich Heine, the only ambassador that Romantic Germany would send to Paris. And it is Baudelaire himself who brings in Heine for us when commenting on his dialogue with the young intellectual and devotee of Pan: "It seems to me," he remarks, "that such immoderate paganism is typical of a man who has read too much and understood too little of Heinrich Heine and that literature of his rotten with materialistic sentimentalism." The harshness of the remark might lead you to suppose that Baudelaire loathes Heine. Quite the contrary. Shortly afterwards he was to speak of him as "this enchanting mind who would be a genius if only he would address himself more often to the divine." And when, in 1865, Jules Janin published a feuilleton scornful of Heine, Baudelaire was seized by "a tremendous rage," as if the article had somehow touched a raw nerve. At once he set about writing a vehement defense of Heine, a poet, he announced, "whom no Frenchman can equal." But the matter got no further than this sudden fury. Later he would write to Michel Lévy: "Then, as soon as I'd written it, and was happy I had, I kept the letter and didn't send it to any of the papers." Fortunately, though, we still have his notes—where one is struck by a sentence that will remain forever the ultimate dismissal of the irritating cult of *bonheur* in all its manifestations: "Je vous plains, monsieur, d'être si facilement heureux"—"I feel sorry for you, monsieur, that you are so easily happy." Attacking Heine, Janin had attacked the whole band of "melancholy and mocking" poets to which, of course, Baudelaire knew he belonged. Hence the strident, exasperated tone of the poet's response, which reads like an act of urgent self-defense. But if Baudelaire's admiration of Heine was such and so great that he actually identified with the German, it follows that the disparaging remarks on Heine in the *École païenne* are not really representative of the poet's mind. And this is the telltale sign that confirms a growing suspicion: Baudelaire is writing the whole piece as if from the point of view of his enemies. From start to finish the thing is tongue-in-cheek. Not only that, but in assuming his enemies' point of view, Baudelaire actually seems to be offering them arguments against himself that are far more effective and biting than any they would have been able to dream up themselves. Only when we have grasped this does the last section of the piece, after the aside on Heine, make sense. Suddenly the spirit is pure Offenbach again: "Let's go back to Olympus. For a while now I've had the whole of Olympus hard at my heels, something that bothers me a great deal; gods are falling on my head like chimney pots. It's like a bad dream, as if I were plunging down into the void and a host of wooden, iron, golden, and silver idols along with me, all chasing after me as I plummet, all shoving me and digging me in the ribs and whacking me over the head." This comic if calamitous vision might well be seen as the final galop of the first half of the nineteenth century, a period which had seen not only the Greek gods invade the psyche once again, but also and following hard after them another huge procession of idols too, their names often quite un-pronounceable. This was the so-called *renaissance orientale*, a process that came out of the work of philologists, who for the first time were translating texts of the greatest importance, while statues, reliefs, and amulets went on and on multiplying in the vast crypts of the museums. The idols were back at last and Europe was under siege, and this at precisely the moment when everyone was singing the praises of Progress and the clarifying powers of Reason. There is thus a wonderfully theatrical timing to the fact that only a few months after Baudelaire's *École païenne*, the *Revue des deux mondes* should publish Heine's *Les Dieux en exil*, which almost amounts to a countermelody to Baudelaire's piece. Heine explains how, before coming back to invade the scene, the pagan gods would have to lead a long and grueling life in hiding, as exiles, "among the owls and toads in the dark hovels of their past splendor." Much of what the world now calls "satanic," he added, was once blessedly pagan. But what happens when the gods come back and show themselves in all the fullness of their sorcery, when Venus once again seduces a mortal man—Tannhäuser, to be precise? We can hardly, as once in the past, say *incessu patuit dea*, and we won't even be able to recognize in the goddess a "noble quiet," as Winckelmann dictates. Rather, Venus will come to meet us as a "demon, that she-devil of a woman who, beneath all her Olympian arrogance and the magnificence of her passion allows us to glimpse *la dame galante*; she's a celestial courtesan perfumed with ambrosia, a divinity *aux camélias*, or as one might say a *déesse entretenue*." In short, the real news is this: the Olympian gods are back and in business, but they live in the *demi-monde*. Complicitous as a pair of jugglers, Baudelaire and Heine conjure together in irreversible combination the reawakening of the gods and the spirit of parody. In so doing they look forward to a state of affairs which is still very much our own today.

But another surprise awaits us in the last paragraphs of the *École païenne*. First there is a blank space, then a brusque change of tone. Suddenly the voice is grave and austere, as if Baudelaire were assuming the attitude of a baroque preacher, an Abraham a Santa Clara raging against the wiles of this world: "To send passion and reason packing," he announces,

is to do literature to death. To repudiate the efforts of the society that came before us, its philosophy and Christianity, would be to commit suicide, to reject the impulse and tools of improvement. To surround oneself exclusively with the seductions of physical art would mean in all probability to lose oneself. In the long run, the very long run, you will see, love, feel only what is beautiful, you will be unable to see anything but beauty. I use the word in its narrow sense. The world will appear to you as merely material. The mechanisms that govern its movement will long remain hidden.

May religion and philosophy return one day, forced into being by the cry of the desperate man. Such will ever be the destiny of those fools who see nothing in nature but rhythms and shapes. Yet at first philosophy will appear to them as no more than an interesting game, an amusing form of gymnastics, a fencing in the void. But how they will be punished for that! Every child whose poetic spirit is overexcited and who is not immediately presented with the stimulating spectacle of a healthy, industrious way of life, who constantly hears tell of glory and of sensual pleasure, whose senses are every day caressed, inflamed, frightened, aroused, and satisfied by works of art, will become the unhappiest of men and make others unhappy too. At twelve he will be pulling up his nanny's skirts, and if some special skill in crime or art doesn't raise him above the crowd, by thirty he will be dying in hospital. Forever inflamed and dissatisfied, his spirit will go abroad in the world, the busy industrious world; it will go abroad, I tell you, like a whore, yelling: Plasticity! Plasticity! Plasticity, that horrible word makes my flesh creep, plasticity has poisoned him, yet he can't live without his poison now. He has banished reason from his heart and, as a just punishment for his crime, reason refuses to return. The happiest thing that can happen to him is that nature strike him with a terrifying call to order. And such, in fact, is the law of life: he who refuses the pure joys of honest activity can feel nothing but the terrible joys of vice. Sin contains its own hell, and from time to time nature says to pain and misery: go and destroy those rebels!

The useful, the true, the good, all that is really

lovable, these things will be unknown to him. Infatuated by his exhausting dream, he will seek to infatuate and exhaust others with it. He will have no time for his mother, his nanny; he will pull his friends to pieces or love them *only for their form;* his wife too, if he has one, he will despise and debase.

The immoderate pleasure he takes in form will drive him to monstrous and unprecedented excesses. Swallowed up by this ferocious passion for the beautiful and the bizarre, the pretty and the picturesque, for the gradations are many, the notions of the true and the just will disappear. The frenetic passion for art is a cancer that eats up everything else; and since the drastic absence of the true and the just is tantamount to the absence of art, man in his entirety will disappear; excessive specialization in a single faculty can only end in emptiness . . . Literature must go back and temper itself once again in a more healthy atmosphere. All too soon it will become clear that a literature that refuses to develop in harmony with science and philosophy is a homicidal and indeed suicidal literature.

The passage is quite astonishing in its ambiguity. It's as though Baudelaire were seeking to couple up his own deepest convictions to the arguments of his most implacable enemies like so many links in the same chain. Reading the piece, one is struck by a suspicion that undermines every word. The overriding impression is that of listening to some theological opponent of Baudelaire's who has somehow been endowed with the poet's own sharp-witted eloquence and deep sense of pathos. Not to mention his irrepressible penchant for the grotesque, evident, for example, where we have the satanic child aesthete pulling up his nanny's skirts. Or where, like some early Monsieur Prudhomme, he appeals to the notion of "a healthy, industrious way of life," and again to "the pure joys of honest activity." It's as if Baudelaire had dropped these hints on purpose to betray what is in fact a perverse game of role reversal. And yet one has to concede that where the text is not playful, its tone austere and stern, the reasoning does carry a grim conviction. It's as if Baudelaire were evoking the figure of some Grand Inquisitor, looking ahead to the pathetic prosecutor who would seek to have *Fleurs du mal* condemned, and transforming him into a literary Joseph de Maistre.

But why resort to such solemn tones? Clearly something extremely menacing was going on—or rather, no, had already happened: the pagan gods had escaped from those niches in literary rhetoric where many presumed they would be forever confined. Now those niches were just empty graves while a group of noble fugitives mingled mockingly with the city crowds. It was Verlaine who would tell us the strange story, and tell it with disarming naturalness, in a juvenile sonnet entitled "Les Dieux":

Vaincus, mais non domptés, exilés mais vivants
Et malgré les édits de l'Homme et ses menaces,
Ils n'ont point abdiqué, crispant leurs mains tenaces
Sur des tronçons de sceptre, et rôdent dans les vents

Beaten, but not tamed, exiled but alive,
Notwithstanding the edicts of man and his threats,
They have not abdicated, their stubborn hands grip
Stumps of scepters, and they wander in the wind.

It's a gloomy vision. The enchanter gods wander like "rapacious ghosts" in a desolate world. The time has come for them to sound their "rebellion against Man," represented, as it turns out, by the eternal pharmacist Homais, who is still "amazed" that he managed to chase the gods off in the first place while presently preparing to burden Humanity with the awkward weight of a capital letter. The sonnet closes with a warning:

Du Coran, des Védas et du Deutéronome,
De tous les dogmes, pleins de rage, tous les dieux
Sont sortis en campagne: Alerte! et veillons mieux.

From the Koran, from the Vedas and from
    Deuteronomy,

From every dogma, full of fury, all the gods
Have come out into the open: Look out! and keep a
   better watch.

It seems that this business of the pagan gods' return oscillates with disturbing ease between vaudeville and gothic novel. But behind these colorful scenes, Baudelaire's unnamed Inquisitor had got wind of a more subtle danger: the emancipation of the aesthetic. It is as if he had foreseen that *aesthetic justification* of the world that only Nietzsche, some years later, would have the temerity to vindicate. The danger he senses lies in the possibility that the category of the Beautiful will free itself from the canonical superiors it has hitherto obeyed: the True and the Good. If this were to happen—and here our Inquisitor is enlightening—"an immoderate pleasure . . . in form" will develop and the "frenetic passion for art" will "eat up everything else," so that in the end nothing will be left, not even art itself. Or, rather, what's left is a merely aesthetic backdrop through which nonetheless (as Valéry put it) "nothingness seeps through." But isn't this the main criticism that has been leveled against the new literature—or at least against great literature—ever since, and starting with Baudelaire himself? The central formulations of the passage—the "immoderate pleasure . . . in form," the "ferocious passion for the beautiful," "frenetic passion for art"—will soon become Nietzsche's "magic of the extreme" and Gottfried Benn's fanaticism for form, which are direct and splendid descendants of Baudelaire himself. We are bound to admit, that is, that the Grand Inquisitor's denunciation casts a long shadow.

Baudelaire's article on the *École païenne* is unique in that in just a few pages of what disguises itself as lively journalism he manages to bring together three elements that had never previously been thought of as inextricably connected: the reawakening of the gods, parody, and what I will be calling "absolute literature," by which I mean literature at its most piercing, its most intolerant of any social trappings. Now let's turn from that to the scenario as it presents itself today. First and most obviously, the gods are still among us. But they are no longer made up of just the one family, however complicated, residing in their vast homes on the slopes of a single mountain. No, now they are multitudes, a teeming crowd in an endless metropolis. It hardly matters that their names are often exotic and unpronounceable, like the names one reads on the doorbells of families of immigrants. The power of their stories is still at work. Yet there is something new and unusual about the situation: this composite tribe of gods now lives *only* in its stories and scattered idols. The way of cult and ritual is barred, either because there is no longer a group of devotees who carry out the ritual gestures, or because even when someone does perform these gestures they stop short. The statues of Śiva and Viṣṇu still drip with offerings, but Varuṇa is a remote and shapeless entity to the Indian of today, while Prajāpati is only to be found in books. And this, one might say, has become the natural condition of the gods: to appear in books—and often in books that few will ever open. Is this the prelude to extinction? Only to the superficial observer. For in the meantime all the powers of the cult of the gods have migrated into a single, immobile and solitary act: that of reading. In the delirium of their love affair with the microchip, people insist on asking tedious questions about the survival of the printed word. While the truly extraordinary phenomenon that is everywhere before us is never even mentioned: the vertiginous and unprecedented concentration of power that has gathered and is gathering in the pure act of reading. That we may be gazing at a screen rather than a page, that the numbers, formulas, and words appear on liquid crystal rather than paper, changes nothing at all: it is still reading. The theatre of the mind seems to have expanded to include rank upon teeming rank of patient signs, all incorporated in this prosthesis which is the computer. Meanwhile, with superstitious confidence, all the sorcery and powers at play are attributed to what appears on the screen, not to the mind that elaborates it—and above all *reads*. Yet what could be more technologically advanced than a transformation that takes place in a totally invisible way, within the mind? The development is dense with hidden consequences. By uniting with the screen the mind, trained or untrained, creates a new kind of Centaur, grows used to seeing itself as an unlimited theatre. Boundless as it is, this apparently new scene resembles nothing more than the vibrant oceanic expanse that the Vedic seers thought of as the mind itself, *manas*. And already in the interstices of that great theatre vast caverns are opening up before our eyes, whence as ever echo the names of the gods.

The world—the time has come to say it, though the news will not be welcome to everyone—has no intention of abandoning enchantment altogether, if only because, even if it could, it would get bored. In the meantime, parody has become a subtle film that has wrapped itself round everything. What in Baudelaire and Heine was just a poisoned splinter of Offenbach has now become the characterizing feature of our age. Today, everything, in whatever form it comes, appears first and foremost as parody. Nature itself is parody. Only afterwards, with great effort and subtlety, it may be that something manages to go *beyond* parody. But it will always be necessary to measure it against its original parodic appearance. And finally: absolute literature. What, as Baudelaire's Grand Inquisitor saw it, was still only the menace in the wings, a serpentine threat, a possible degeneration, has turned out after all to be literature itself. Or at least, the only kind of literature that I have come here to talk to you about.

II

Mental Waters

The gods manifest themselves intermittently along with the flow and ebb of what Aby Warburg referred to as the "mnemonic wave." This expression, which appears at the opening of a posthumously published essay on Burckhardt and Nietzsche, alludes to those successive surges of the memory that a civilization experiences in relation to its past, in this case that part of the West's past which is inhabited by the Greek gods. This wave has been a constant throughout European history, sometimes rolling in, sometimes trickling out, and the two writers Warburg chooses to talk about can be seen as representing polar opposites in their reactions to that wave at a moment when it was decidedly on the flood. Burckhardt and Nietzsche were similar, Warburg claims, in being necromancers in relation to the past. Yet their attitudes toward the "mnemonic wave" were quite different. Burckhardt was determined to the end to keep a strict distance between himself and that wave, if only because he was aware of the danger—indeed, the terror that must come with it. Nietzsche on the other hand abandons himself to the wave, *becomes* himself the wave, right up to the day when he would sign some brief letters posted from Turin with the name Dionysus. One of those letters was addressed to Burckhardt and concluded with these words: "Now you, sir, you are our great, our greatest, master: for I, together with Ariadne, must only be the golden equilibrium of all things, at every stage there are those who are above us . . ." Signed: Dionysus. But we can safely say that ever since Ficino, Poliziano, and Botticelli frequented the Orti Oricellari of early-fifteenth-century Florence, the story of our dealings with the gods has been one long succession of peaks and troughs. Where the lowest point was probably a moment in eighteenth-century France when, with breezy and derisive self-assurance, the childish Greek fables, the barbaric Shakespeare, and the sordid biblical tales were all summarily dismissed as no more than the work of a shrewd priesthood determined to suffocate any potentially enlightened minds in their cradles. Indeed, it was sometimes the case that all three targets would be mocked by the selfsame pen: Voltaire's, for example. In the course of this long, tortuous, and dangerously deceptive story, the pagan gods might assume any sort of shape, disguise, or function. Often they were reduced to a merely papery existence, as moral allegories, personifications, prosopopoeias, and other contrivances of rhetoric's arsenal. Sometimes they were secret ciphers, as in the writings of the alchemists.

Sometimes they were the merest pretext for lyricism, no more than an evocative sound. But whatever the form, we almost always have the feeling that they are not being given free rein, as if, without anything's being said, people were afraid of them, as if the master of the house—the hand that writes—regarded them as prestigious but ungovernable guests, and hence to be kept under discreet observation. Long euphemized and tightly bridled in literary texts, the gods ran wild in painting. Thanks to its wordless nature, which allows it to be immoral without coming out and saying as much, the painted image was able to restore the gods to their glamorous and terrifying apparitions as simulacra. Hence a long and uninterrupted *banquet of the gods* runs parallel with Western history from Botticelli and Giovanni Bellini, through Guido Reni and Bernini, Poussin and Rembrandt (*The Rape of Persephone* would itself suffice), Saraceni and Furini and Dossi, right through to Tiepolo. For almost four centuries these were our gods: silently shining out from picture galleries, parks, private studies. So that if we were to take away the representations of the pagan gods from the paintings of the fifteenth century through to the end of the eighteenth, we would create a vortex that would draw a great deal else down with it, and the development of art in those centuries would seem disconnected and schizoid. It is as if, in short, the passage from one style to another, one period to another, were something that was secretly handed down through the gods and their emissaries, whether Nymphs or Satyrs or winged messengers.

But above all Nymphs. It was this band of female and immensely long-lived, though not immortal, creatures who were to be the most faithful when it came to assisting metamorphoses in style. Announced for the first time in fifteenth-century Florence by the breeze that ruffled their robes (and it was a "brise imaginaire," as Warburg points out), they have never ceased to make eyes at us from fountains and fireplaces, ceilings, columns, balconies, decorative niches, and balustrades. And they weren't just an excuse for eroticism, the pretext for having a breast or a naked belly grab a place in our field of vision, though they were sometimes that too. The Nymphs are heralds of a form of knowledge, perhaps the most ancient, certainly the most dangerous: possession. Apollo was the first to find this out when he beset and then chased away the Nymph Telphusa, solitary guardian of an "unblemished place" (*chóros apémon*), as the Homeric hymn puts it, in the vicinity of Delphi. He had come there looking for a place to found an oracle for those who lived in the Peloponnese, the islands, and "those who dwell in Europe"—and this is the first text to refer to Europe as a geographic entity, though here it still means only central and northern Greece. First Apollo encounters the Nymph Telphusa, then the female dragon Python. Both protected a "spring of sweet waters," as the hymn says, using the same expression twice. And with both Nymph and dragon Apollo uses the same words when he announces his intentions. For both were manifestations of a power that had split itself in two, appearing now as an enchanting young girl, now as a huge coiled serpent. One day the two figures would be reunited in Melusina, but for the moment what linked them was the thing they were protecting: water that issued from the ground—water at once wise and powerful. Before anything else, Apollo was the first invader and usurper of this knowledge that did not belong to him: a liquid, fluid knowledge on which the god would now impose his own meter. From that day on, one of the names he let his worshipers call him was Apollo Telphusios.

Nýmphē means both "girl ready for marriage" and "spring of water." Each meaning protects and encloses the other. To approach a Nymph is to be seized, possessed by something, to immerse oneself in an element at once soft and unstable, that may be thrilling or may equally well prove fatal. In the *Phaedrus*, Socrates was proud to describe himself as a *nymphóleptos*, one "captured by the Nymphs." But Hylas, Heracles' lover, was swallowed up by a pool of water inhabited by the Nymphs and never reappeared. The Nymph, whose arm drew him towards her to kiss him, "thrust him down in the middle of the whirlpool." Nothing is more terrible, nothing more precious than the knowledge that comes from the Nymphs. But what are these waters of theirs? Only in late pagan times do we get a clue, when, in his *De antro nympharum*, Porphyry cites a hymn to Apollo which speaks of the *noeròn udátōn*, the "mental waters" that the Nymphs brought as a gift to Apollo. Once conquered, the Nymphs offered themselves. The Nymph is the quivering, sparkling, vibrating, *mental matter* of which the simulacrum, the image, the *eídōlon* is made. It is the very stuff of literature. Every time the Nymph shows herself, this divine material that molds itself into epiphanies and enthrones itself in the mind, this power that precedes and upholds the word, begins once again to throb. The moment that power makes itself manifest, form will follow, adjusting and composing itself with the power's flow.

The most recent, majestic, and dazzling celebration of the Nymph is to be found in *Lolita*, the story of a *nymphóleptos*, Professor Humbert Humbert, an "enchanted hunter" who enters the realm of the Nymphs in pursuit of a pair of white bobby socks and another pair of heart-shaped spectacles. Nabokov, a master when it came to filling his books with secrets so plainly visible and even obvious that nobody could see them, states his tormented hero's motives in a splendid tribute to the Nymphs only ten pages into the novel when, with his lexicographer's scrupulosity, he explains how "between the age limits of nine and fourteen there occur maidens who, to certain bewitched travelers, twice or thrice older than they, reveal their true nature which is not human, but nymphic (that is demoniac); and these chosen creatures I propose to designate as 'nymphets.'" Although the word "nymphet" was to enjoy an astonishing future, mainly in the ecumenical community of pornography, not many readers realized that in those few lines Nabokov was actually offering the key to the novel's enigma. Lolita is a Nymph who wanders among the motels of the Midwest, an "immortal daemon disguised as a female child" in a world where the *nymphóleptoi* will, like Humbert Humbert, have to choose between being thought of as criminals or psychopaths. From the "mental waters" of the Nymphs to the gods themselves, the passage is an easy one. If only because, when the gods made their forays down to earth, it was more often than not the Nymphs rather than the humans who attracted them. The Nymph is the *medium* in which gods and adventurous men may meet. But how can one recognize the gods? On this point writers have always been blessedly bold. They have always acted as if alluding to an enlightened observation of Ezra Pound's: "No apter metaphor having been found for certain emotional colours, I assert that the Gods exist." The writer is one who *sees* those "emotional colours."

As for the esoteric truth of *Lolita*, this Nabokov crammed into a tiny sentence buried like a splinter of diamond in the overall mass of the novel: "The science of nympholepsy is a precise science." What he did not say is that it was this "precise science" that, even more than his beloved entomology, he had been practicing his life long: literature.

The Nymphs clear the way—but other divine figures may burst into literature. So it is that in rare moments of pure incandescence the gods themselves can still take on a presence that leaves us speechless, overwhelmed, as the encounter with an unknown traveler may overwhelm and bewilder. This is what happened to Hölderlin. Born in 1770, at the close of what was for the gods the most arid and impervious of ages, he seemed from earliest childhood to be waiting for the "mnemonic wave," which eventually crashed onto him like a breaker on rocks. But one mustn't imagine that Hölderlin was alone in possessing this sensibility, though the form of his hymns would indeed be unique. When Hölderlin was still a tutor in the house of Diotima—otherwise Susette Gontard, wife of a Frankfurt banker—and before he had been dazzled by Apollo, he would receive a visit, in October 1797, from the twenty-three-year-old Siegfried Schmid. For two hours they talked about poetry in the attic room where Hölderlin lived. Having returned to Basle, Schmid wrote the poet a letter still pulsing with arcane enthusiasm. And he added a few lines of verse, including this couplet:

> Alles ist Leben, beseelt uns der Gott, unsichtbar,
>> empfundnes.
>> Leise Berührungen sind's; aber von heiliger Kraft.

> All is life, if God animates us, invisible, felt.
>> They are light touches, but of sacred power.

It is hard to imagine how the essential tone, not just of one person but of the whole poetic psyche of the moment, could have been better or more soberly described. And at once we have an example of that "clarity of representation" (*Klarheit der Darstellung*) that, as Hölderlin himself would put it, "is as native and natural to us as the fire in the sky was to the Greeks." Before the names themselves appear, then, before Greece rises dizzyingly up with its divinities and their noisy retinue, we have these "light touches" which alert us to the presence of an unnamed god. This was the experience from which all the rest followed, and that each would then elaborate after his fashion. Two years before Schmid's letter Herder had already been wondering whether that new creature everyone was talking about—the nation—didn't need a mythology of its own, and he looked forward to a resurrection of the Eddic myths. Schiller replied that he preferred to stay with the Greeks and their myths, and hence be "related to a bygone age, remote and ideal, since reality could only spoil it." A few months later and Friedrich Schlegel would be asking himself whether it mightn't be possible to think up "a new mythology"—a fatal idea this, which would do the rounds of Europe until it got as far as Leopardi in remote Recanati. Leopardi was certainly favorably inclined to the "antique fables"; they were the mysterious remnants of a world where reason hadn't yet been able to unleash the full effects of its lethal power, a power that "renders all the objects to which it turns its attention small and vile and empty, destroys the great and the beautiful and even, as it were, existence itself, and thus is the true mother and cause of nothingness, so that the more it grows, the smaller things get." But Leopardi was too clear-sighted, his ear too finely tuned, not to appreciate that the "antique mythology," if dragged bodily into the modern world like so many plaster busts, "can no longer produce the effects it once had." Indeed, "in applying anew the same or similar fictions, whether to ancient matters, or to modern subjects or meaner times, there is always something arid or false in them, because even when, from the point of view of beauty, imagination, marvel, etc., all is perfect, still the persuasion of the past is missing." In short, we moderns lack conviction; we don't experience an inextricable tangling of the "antique fables" with the gestures and beliefs shared by our community, "since though we have inherited their literature, we did not inherit Greek and Roman religion along with it." Without this bedrock, it follows that "Italian or modern writers who use the antique fables in the manner of the ancients, go beyond a just imitation and exaggerate." The result is an "affectation, a crude sham," a clumsy posturing, "pretending to be ancient Italians and concealing as far as possible the fact that they are modern Italians." This is Leopardi at his most unforgiving, passing what seems to be final sentence not only on all romantic appropriations of the "antique fables" but on the whole verbal armory of those future Parnassians and symbolists whose appeal to the gods was above all a shield against the vulgarity of the shopkeeper. Yet despite this biting dismissal of all would-be "new mythologies," Leopardi was nevertheless to give us a sympathetic and farsighted justification for the use of the "antique fables." They are useful—no, they are precious—when it comes to escaping the asphyxia of our own time, with respect to which the poet can only be a ceaseless saboteur, since "everything can be at home in this century but poetry." And here one might say that Leopardi is setting up a generous plea that might be used in defense of Flaubert, to absolve him from the one sin he can be accused of: not, of course, the immorality of *Madame Bovary*, but the noble shipwreck that is *Salammbô*. By all means let us hear Leopardi's peroration:

> Let's forgive the modern poet, then, if he follows antique ways, if he adopts the language, style, and manner of the ancients, and likewise if he uses the antique fables, etc., if he pretends to have ancient opinions, if he prefers antique customs, usages, and events, if he imposes on his poetry the character of a bygone age, if he seeks, in short, to be, so far as his spirit and nature are concerned, or to seem ancient. Let's forgive the poet and the poetry that don't sound modern, that are not contemporary to this century, for to be contemporary to this century, is, or necessarily involves, not being a poet, not being poetry.

Leopardi was speaking of the writers who *named* the ancient gods. But there is one writer of whom we may suspect that he *saw* the gods *enargeîs*, in all their vividness: Hölderlin. In comparison with his contemporaries, what happened with Hölderlin—as Schmid's couplet so delicately announces—was something far more radical. One needed to go beyond and *behind* the gods, to arrive at the pure divine, or rather the "immediate," as Hölderlin was to write one day in a

dazzling comment on Pindar. It is the immediate that
escapes not only men but the gods too: "The immediate, strictly speaking, is as impossible for the gods as it
is for men." Hölderlin is referring here to the lines
where Pindar speaks of the *nómos basileús*, the "law
that reigns over all, mortals and immortals alike."
Whatever else it might be, the divine is certainly the
thing that imposes with maximum intensity the sensation of being alive. This is the immediate: but pure
intensity, as a continuous experience, is "impossible,"
overwhelming. To preserve its sovereignty, the immediate must come across to us through the law. If life
itself is the supreme unlivable, the law, which allows
both mortals and immortals to "distinguish between
different worlds" is what transmits life's nature to us.
At least if—staying with Hölderlin—what we mean by
"nature" is that which "is above the gods of the West
and the East," and which, as he says, is "generated
out of sacred chaos." At this point Heidegger would
later ask: "How can *cháos* and *nómos* be brought
together?" It is here perhaps that we come to the bold
provocative core of Hölderlin's poetry: never before
nor after him would chaos and law be brought so close
together, obliged to acknowledge, as in Vedic India—
where Dakṣa, the supreme minister of the law, is son
of Aditi, the Unlimited One, and Aditi is daughter of
Dakṣa—a relationship of reciprocal generation. Chaos
generates the law, but only the law will allow us to

gain access to chaos. The unapproachable immediate is chaos—and "chaos is the sacred itself," adds Heidegger, and at once he goes on to develop a modulation that would have seemed obvious to the theorists of the *nirukta*, yet sounds incongruous to Western linguists, from the verb *ent-setzen*, "to shift," to the neuter *das Entsetzliche*, "the awesome," which is used to define the sacred: "The sacred is the awesome [*das Entsetzliche*] itself." Then comes a sentence which is rather mysterious: "But its awesomeness remains hidden in the mildness of this light embrace." Words which clearly—and it was a clarity Heidegger was certainly after—set out to echo Rilke:

Denn das Schöne ist nichts
als des Schrecklichen Anfang, den wir noch grade
ertragen.

Since the beautiful is only
The beginning of the awesome, as we are barely able to
endure it.

But at the same time too we are reminded once more of the words of the young Schmid: "They are light touches, but of sacred power." Between Schmid and Rilke, between 1797 and 1923, a spark was struck and a fire lit that would prove inextinguishable. This was the period in which the epiphany of a multiplicity of gods went hand in hand with the overturning of established forms, a prolonged contact with the "sacred chaos," the emancipation of literature from all the authorities it had previously obeyed.

But, even when it comes to this new vision of chaos, it would be misleading to suppose that it was Hölderlin's exclusive and peculiar property. On the contrary, we can even identify the year in which chaos triumphs. It is 1800. Hölderlin was writing "Wie wenn am Feiertage . . . ," lines that wouldn't reach his readers until 1910, when Hellingrath published the poem. Here we find the opening precept: "das Heilige sei mein Wort"—"may the sacred be my word"; here, three lines on, the poet speaks of nature as "reawakened with the clash of arms"; here, immediately afterward, the "sacred chaos" is named. Now in April of 1800, in the fifth issue of the Athenaeum, you would have found Friedrich Schlegel's "Conversation on Poetry." And since, in Schlegel, we are not, as with Hölderlin, listening to an indomitably individual voice, but to the expression of a group of kindred spirits—a Bund that went from Novalis to Schelling—we are now obliged to acknowledge that certain words have taken on a resonance hitherto unheard of. Suddenly the word "chaos" gathers exhilarating connotations. Instead of being opposed to form, its enemy, it seems to suggest a higher form, of fragrant vividness, where finally nature and artifice mix together to be separated no more, in the "beautiful muddle of the imagination." And looking for a symbol that might suggest the "original chaos of human nature," Schlegel admitted that he knew of none better than the "shining tangle of the ancient gods." This, then, is the connection by means of which, from now on, the reappearance of the ancient gods can be seen as accomplice and instigator of that breaking-down and recasting of forms that characterizes the most daring literature. As if formal experimentation and divine epiphany had made a pact—and the one could now step forward in place of the other and say: *larvatus prodeo*, I proceed disguised.

What is unique about Hölderlin, then, is not his perception of a new presence of the ancient gods—all of the *Athenaeum* group shared that perception and declared it as a new article of faith—but his focusing on the *difference* that the gods had acquired in now manifesting themselves to the moderns. This, at bottom, is *the* point at which history impresses itself on all that is, the point at which we are forced to acknowledge that time, in its mere rolling by, has changed something in the world's very essence.

When Hölderlin names the gods, when he writes that the god is "near / And hard to grasp," we sense he is speaking of a force that precedes, exceeds, and looms far above every poetic vision. His perception of this force was, we might even say, too precise. But no one more than Hölderlin knew how very different that god was from the god that had appeared to the Greeks. And this is the subject of his most arduous speculations, from the letters to Böhlendorff to the fragments on *Antigone*. For the Greeks, the god appears as Apollo appeared to the Argonauts in the words of Apollonius Rhodius:

Now, when the immortal light has still to rise, yet all is no longer quite dark but a light glow has spread across the night, and this is when those who awake say that the day is dawning, at that time they hove into port in the deserted island of Thynias, and exhausted from their efforts climbed down on the shore. And unto them the son of Leto, who was coming from Lycia and on his way to visit the innumerable people of the Hyperboreans, appeared; golden curls each side of his head flowed down in clusters as he went; in his left hand he held a silver bow, on his shoulders hung a quiver; and beneath his feet the whole island trembled, and the waves rose on the beach. Those who saw him felt an uncontrollable dismay [*thámbos améchanon*]. And no one dared look the god directly in his beautiful eyes. They stood stock still, head bowed; but he, far away, passed over the sea through the air.

Towering as Poussin's Orion, yet suspended over an empty sea, just as the dawn spreads its first light,

43

absorbed and unconcerned: such is the god. He barely touches the heroes, whom he could easily trample underfoot. Instead it is the earth and the sea that quake. What can these men do? They listen to the words of Orpheus: "Take courage, and let us call this island sacred to the Apollo of the Dawn, for he appeared to us all, while walking in the dawn." Then he invites his companions to offer a sacrifice to the gods. What could be more straightforward? Everybody has the same vision, all feel the same dismay, all help build the same altar. But what happens if there are no Argonauts, all sharing the same experience? What if no one knows how to build an altar? What if no one dares make an offering? This was Hölderlin's secret thought. And concealed within it was another, more secret still: not only has our way of welcoming the god changed, but the form in which the god himself appears is different: "we cannot have something the same" as the Greeks had, Hölderlin confides to Böhlendorff. If only because—he adds a few lines later and with sudden harshness—"we leave the realm of the living tight-lipped, mute, shut up in some box or other." It is not for us "consumed in the flames to expiate the flame that we could not subdue." And this is "the tragic for us": this meanness in our deaths.

Hölderlin knows the gods can't reappear in a circle of statues over which the heavy curtain of history will suddenly rise. That was the neoclassical vision, which

Hölderlin was the first to distance himself from. No, like figures on a carousel gods and men follow the back-and-forth of a secret movement that takes them now closer together, now further apart. Everything lies in grasping the law that governs that movement. Hölderlin calls it "turning back to nativeness" (*vaterländische Umkehr*). His most strenuous and obscure speculations, which still remain to be fathomed two hundred years on, are dedicated to that movement. Of these, I wish to mention one trait in particular: Hölderlin doesn't speak of a situation where gods and men start to meet each other once again. Quite the contrary: in a scenario that he compares to that of the Thebes of Oedipus, "in the plague and in the confusion of the senses, and the general quickening of the spirit of divination," in an age, what's more, that Hölderlin then surprisingly describes as *müssig*, which is to say at once "vain" and "idle," god and man, "in order that the world's flow might not be interrupted and *the memory of the divinities not be extinguished, communicate through the form, oblivious to everything, of infidelity,* since divine infidelity is what is most easily retained." Far from renewing an old relationship, gods and men immediately set about deceiving each other. "In such a moment man forgets himself and the god and turns around [*kehrt . . . um*], in a sacred way for sure, like a traitor." So this new epiphany of the gods proves to be extremely ambiguous, a sort of salvation to be won only through deceit. The place we live in is thus the no-man's-land where a double betrayal, a double infidelity, is going on: the gods' betrayal of men and men's betrayal of the gods. And it is in this place that the poetic word must now take form. There's no question, then, of developing new mythologies, as if a mythology were a kind of fancy dress that made life more exciting. The very idea that mythology is something *one invents* suggests an unpardonable arrogance, as if myth were at our beck and call. Rather, it is we, the will of each and every one of us, that are at the beck and call of myth.

"We dream of originality and autonomy, we believe we are saying only what is new, and all this is no more than a reaction, a sort of mild vendetta against the state of servitude in which we find ourselves with regard to the ancient world." Straightforward as they are drastic, the words are to be found in one of Hölderlin's prose fragments. And a few lines further on he explains how in our relationship with the past a powerful spell is at work, a spell that still has us in its thrall, so that the whole of the past appears to us as "an almost limitless prehistory which we can never become fully conscious of, either through education or experience, and which acts upon us and oppresses us." It is not only enthusiasm and the "fire in the sky" we need to recover now. Hölderlin had already tried that—and said only this of the experience: "we almost lost the power of speech in a foreign land," words over which looms the shadow of Apollo who overwhelmed him in France. No, now it's a question of recovering "Western sobriety," that "clarity of representation" that the Greeks, born of oriental ardor, discovered as a, for them, exotic splendor in the verse of Homer—but which for us Hesperians, the modern Westerners, dry and blinkered as we are, is our native land, a place we must set out to rediscover, betraying the gods. But "in a sacred way for sure."

What is this "Junonic Western sobriety" that is our natural heritage—and as such the most difficult of characteristics to identify, since "what is natural to us must be learned no less than what is foreign"? Hölderlin doesn't say. He offers neither illustrations nor examples. Yet we sense that, though rarely found unalloyed, it is a constant if undeclared feature of literature in the West—something that we find in every age and in every register. When it asserts itself, it has the authority of a pulse beat. And then we are astonished by its sheer obviousness. It is what happens when we turn to Henry Vaughan and read:

> I saw Eternity the other night
> Like a great *Ring* of pure and endless light,
>   All calm, as it was bright.

Many have *seen* eternity, but only Vaughan, and he only in this poem, saw it "the other night," as if it were an old acquaintance, or some traveler freshly arrived from abroad. Crucial here is the complete absence of preliminaries, the lightning suddenness with which the vision is introduced—and at the same time the sobriety in recording the event, as if one were to say: "There was a brawl the other night at the corner of X and Y." And even more than "Eternity" the crucial word is "night," for it determines the three rhymes. Might one speculate that what Hölderlin meant by the expression "Western sobriety" was something that calls to us from beyond enthusiasm, beyond that impulse that draws us to mingle with the gods, but which can disappoint, since it cannot "preserve God through purity and by making distinctions"? But even this is still only a definition by negatives. Otherwise we can merely observe that immediately after the elliptical formulations of the "turning back to native-ness," Hölderlin's style becomes ever more rugged, abrupt, broken. Until finally it eases out into the pensive, boundless uniformity of the last lyrics, where Scardanelli takes on the ceremonial role of him who stamps on the seal.

Towards the end Hölderlin abandons theory. If he has to pass judgment, he writes that something is *prächtig*, "splendid": "life" itself, or even "the sky." He now asks no more than to observe and name nature in its most common manifestations, though sometimes too in its most rare. Like the comets: "Would I like to be a comet? I think so. For they have the speed of the birds; they flower in fire, and are like children, in their purity. To wish for anything greater is not within man's reach."

III

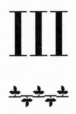

Incipit parodia

Of the ideas that were to fashion the twentieth century in ways for the most part disastrous, one that stands out above the others, so far-reaching and indeed immense were its consequences, is the idea of the *good* community, where relationships between individuals are strong and a powerful solidarity is founded on common feeling. Nazi Germany was the most drastic manifestation of this idea, Soviet Russia the most long-lived and territorially vast. And the world is still full of those who will champion this idea. Why is the phenomenon so tenacious? On what does it depend? First and most crucially, as is ever the way, on a desire: many still feel that a community, any community, in the sense of a group—be it the merest criminal association—where much is held in *common* and where ties between individuals are meaningful, is the ideal place to live. So intense is their desire to live in such a community that the reasons for and nature of those ties hardly seem important. What matters is that they be strong and close-knit. And this when all the evidence before us should at least prompt us to inquire: might there not be something pernicious in the very idea of community, at least when it manifests itself, as has frequently been the case, in a world where technology has extended its grip over the whole planet? This is the crux of the matter: are community and technology somehow incompatible? Not in the sense that a community cannot be established in a technology-driven world—we know all too well that it can—but in the sense that once established, such a community can only lead to results that are radically different from those originally intended.

The question is an urgent one and demands a response, if only because such responses as it gets can prevent or precipitate one of the many massacres someone is forever on the brink of perpetrating. Each one of these disasters comes fitted out, like some grotesque puppet, in peculiarly local dress and regional arguments; but once the many vernaculars have been translated into the lingua franca, the question is always the same, so much so that it has now invaded a vast area of our field of vision. It's an ancient question, whose beginnings, as Italo Calvino once slyly remarked, swing back and forth, according to one's point of view, "between the end of the Paleolithic and the beginnings of the Industrial Revolution." And it's a question that has to do with the whole. Clumsy as it may be, the word "globalization" at least has the merit, constructed as it is around the word "globe," the largest conceivable whole, of being symptomatic. Now, communities conceived as a whole—or "holistic societies," as Louis Dumont referred to them—have been the norm in the history of humanity, in all its phases and all its many forms, while the society based on technology stands out as an extraordinary novelty. Here all kinds of equivocations raise their heads: on the one hand, it would be absurd to blame community, as such, for the terrible crimes that plagued the last century; on the other hand, one cannot help wondering whether the traditional criticisms leveled at the technological society—that it fragments and atomizes, leaving people rootless and alienated—are not in fact aimed at a false target, or at least at something that is no more than a façade. Meanwhile behind that façade another powerful holistic machine is at work, a machine as big now as the planet itself and intent on weaving together a community, exclusive of all others, yet capable of accommodating all those others within itself like so many Indian reservations, some of them seething with natives and vast as subcontinents. It will be obvious that in some respects this new entity is radically different from those that came before it. Here for the first time the natural world is no longer that which surrounds and encloses a community, but that which is itself enclosed. As in China the park of the Son of Heaven is home to examples of every kind of living creature, but only as samples and emblems, so the

Earth is now no longer the place "on which the altar is circumscribed," but has itself become that circumscribed place whence the materials for our experiments can be collected. No one knows now how to invoke it so that "dressed in Agni [Fire] the black-kneed Earth" might make us "resplendent, keen." And no one could now claim to recognize in its fragrance the same scent "that at the marriage of Suryā, Daughter of the Sun, impregnated the immortals on the edge of the times." It was then that "as a horse frees itself from dust, the Earth shook off the peoples who had dwelt on her since her birth." Those motes of scattered dust now have the earth in their grip, yet have almost forgotten how to caress the body of the "golden breasted" woman to whom they long clung as parasites. This new and boundless community is governed by rules based on phantoms and procedures—rules no less binding than those of ancient communities. Before such an all-embracing power could establish itself, a coup d'état had to take place, a long and extremely slow coup d'état by which the brain's analogical pole was gradually supplanted by the digital pole, the pole of substitution, of exchange, of convention, on which are based both language itself and the vast network of procedures in which we now live. This phenomenon, at once psychic, economic, social, and logical, is the consequence of a revolution that has been going on for thousands of years, and is still going on: the one truly permanent revolution we know of. Its Zeus is the algorithm. From this revolution all else follows. Yet it is a process still largely unrecognized, and perhaps we cannot even hope to recognize it in its entirety, since we are still immersed in it—submersed, even. In which case the questions we should be asking lie elsewhere: Is the technological community compatible with itself? Or will it be overwhelmed by the very process that brought it into being?

Certainly whoever it was who wrote the short text that usually goes by the name *The First Systematic Program of German Idealism* could hardly have been thinking of all this. Was it Schelling? Or Hegel? People still argue the point. The manuscript has been dated at around 1797 and was found among Hegel's papers and in his handwriting. In any event, whether Schelling or Hegel, the author was struck by an idea that he not unreasonably declared to be new: "I shall speak of an idea that so far as I know of has never occurred to anyone before: we must have a new mythology." Now then, this idea belongs to the vast web of implication that spreads out from the word "community"—a fact that did not escape the unknown author, who continued thus: "So long as we are unable to make our ideas aesthetic, which is to say mythological, they can be of no interest to the *people*." There it is, the fatal word "people," a word that is no more than a stronger formulation of the more subdued "community." The assumption looks forward to the premise Nietzsche would one day announce in characteristically peremptory tones: "Without myth every civilization loses its healthy and creative natural force: only a horizon drawn by myths can hold together a process of civilization in a single unit."

Like a whisper, or a light-footed messenger, the idea of the "new mythology" would set out from this obscure manuscript buried in Hegel's papers to visit other minds. Friedrich Schlegel's, for example. A few months later, on the pages of the *Athenaeum*, he would be writing: "We don't have a mythology. But I am telling you: we are about to have one, or rather, for a long time now we have been working hard to produce one." As so often, Friedrich Schlegel is displaying a remarkable effrontery here: true, the essential question is briefly illuminated, but immediately the mind is obliged to go a step further and ask: can one really "work hard to produce" a mythology, in the way one might produce a literary review? There is something strident in the words, but Schlegel doesn't want to dwell on that. Nobly ebullient as his concepts become increasingly vague, he goes on: "The new mythology must be elaborated from the most profound depths of the spirit; it must be the most artistic of all works of art, since it will have to embrace all others, be a new riverbed and recipient for the ancient eternal and original spring of poetry, and be itself the infinite poem that contains hidden within it the germ of all other poems." The final thrust runs as follows: "You may smile, perhaps, at this mystic poetry and the disorder that such a throng and profusion of poetry would produce. But the supreme beauty, nay, the supreme order, is still and only the beauty of chaos, and to be precise of a chaos waiting only for the contact of love to open out into a world of harmony, like the world of ancient mythology and ancient poetry. For mythology and poetry are one and the same, indivisible." More than a critic, Friedrich Schlegel was a formidable literary strategist. He had a talent for the impetuous and ambiguous—the which he deployed so as to illuminate one way forward while obscuring a great many others. One day it would be plain that that way was in fact the chosen path toward a literature Schlegel himself was born not to practice but to prophesy—something that I shall be calling absolute literature.

There was no solid theory to what Schlegel was suggesting. His comments more closely resemble a lightning military strike than a piece of reasoning. People must be made to accept an act of appropriation. The whole of mythology was brusquely annexed to poetry. Henceforth the gods would no longer be mere inert material dragged out of rhetoric's warehouse to decorate the friezes and pediments of neoclassicism, but the very stuff and spring of literature itself. And, like a gambler who keeps on raising the stakes, Schlegel adds: there is no question of speaking of just the one mythology, for "insofar as they are profound, beautiful, and wise, the other mythologies must also be reawakened to hasten the formation of the new mythology." *This* is the decisive move: to rend the heavens to the East and let a swarm of unknown divinities settle on the European scene with the same rights as the Olympians: "Oh, that the treasures of the Orient were as accessible to us as those of classical Greece! What new springs of poetry might flow to us from India if only some German artists with the universality, the depth of comprehension, the genius of translation that is naturally theirs, could take advantage of the opportunity that this ever more brutal and obtuse nation little knows how to seize. It is in the East that we must look for the Romantic supreme." This sentence was indeed the reckless supreme of the Romantic endeavor. But the Romantics would never get to the Orient. Rather, they were themselves the Orient of Europe, an Orient whose music rang out on piano keys. The Orient in the literal sense remained far away and was allowed to filter through only with prudence. But this should hardly surprise us: it is still far away today and continues to provoke an unspoken fear whenever its texts and images are approached. Not that Schlegel didn't make an honest attempt: a few years after the piece in *Athenaeum* and having taught himself some Sanskrit, he was to publish a book called *On the Language and Wisdom of the Indians*. And yet we find too little in those pages to justify such an ambitious title, and only as a nostalgic farewell does Schlegel allow himself, in passing, as it were, the fine definition of mythology as "the densest weave of the human spirit." This sudden paralysis of an otherwise febrile mind can be attributed to a hidden motive that we haven't as yet touched on: there is a perennial duplicity in the early Romantics whenever they talk of the gods, the myths and mythology. At first the subject had been presented in purely literary terms: the gods and the mythological fabric around them (only the ancient gods? only the Greek? or the modern as well? and the Oriental too?) offered the possibility for a grandiose reshuffling of the literary pack. It was as if forms left barren by the Enlightenment were longing to take in these divine guests, not just as ornamental walk-ons now, but in all the fullness of their powers. At the same time it was clear to everybody that evoking the gods meant evoking the communities that had celebrated their cults. So the Romantics looked around outside their small kingdoms, countries thrown into turmoil by the Napoleonic whirlwind, and couldn't find anything that would serve their purpose. Neither the society that was falling apart nor the one that seemed ready to form had anything to do with those antique communities that had experienced the adventures of the gods in the Mysteries, or, at the end, in that ceremony that was Greek tragedy. At which point Romantic eloquence ran dry. They drew back as if afraid of being surprised by the police, and chose to let a convenient curtain come down upon the scene. Speculations about the "new mythology" soon petered out.

All the same, a fuse had been lit and would continue to burn, winding slowly and tortuously back and forth for the whole century. The sulphurous smell of that fuse was strongest round one name in particular: Dionysus. Last of the Olympians, a foreigner, an Oriental, a dissolver of ties, Dionysus set foot in Germany after a long absence from Europe, an absence that stretched back to the times of Pico and Ficino, Poliziano and Botticelli in a Florence where he was worshiped as the god of mysteries and divine rapture. All those centuries ago the memory of one plain and cutting remark of Plato's had been enough to get the god's cult going: "Madness is superior to temperance [*sophrosýnē*], because the latter has a merely human origin, while the former belongs to the divine." The Germany of the early nineteenth century, however, was a great deal more shy and prudish, so much so that the illustrious translator of Homer Johann Heinrich Voss rendered the "nocturnal orgies" of Dionysus as his "light entertainments."

How much more astonishing, then, is the naturalness with which Dionysus turns up in the poetry of Hölderlin. At the beginning of "Brot und Wein" it is the night that takes our breath away, in eighteen lines all in the present tense. Rarely has the pure power of naming showed itself so very clearly. Then from the isthmus of Corinth comes Dionysus, "the god who arrives unexpected." And this time he's not the last god, but the penultimate; he comes before him who "brought to completion and closed, consoling, the celestial feast." The last, unnamed, is Christ. Such an exalted and silent concentration of the divine is not easily borne. Withdrawing it from man is an ironic act of grace on the part of the gods:

> Denn nicht immer vermag ein schwaches Gefäss sie
>   zu fassen,
> Nur zu Zeiten erträgt göttliche Fülle der Mensch.

> As a weak vase isn't always able to receive it,
> Only at intervals can man bear divine fullness.

So, no sooner was he back than the "advent god" had to go into hiding again, in the form the gods had come to prefer: among the pages of scholars. And, if possible, of scholars under fierce attack from those of their colleagues who were always ready to smell out the menacing footprint of the god in a forest of texts and, like Pentheus at Thebes, stop him getting through. In 1808, a few months after the suicide of his beloved Karoline von Günderode, Friedrich Creuzer published, in Latin, his *Dionysus*, which he opened by saying that in the "almost infinite" multitude of the Greek fables, "ulla unquam tam late patuit, quam illa, quae per Bacchicarum rerum amplissima spatia ducit"—"none appeared so late as the one that tells the Dionysiac adventures, which cover so vast a space."

And immediately he pays homage to the vast *Dionysiaca* of the poet Nonnus, a work that for centuries had lain "situ squaloreque obsita," "covered in dirt and debris." As if to insinuate that since ancient times the name Dionysus had been the object of a Western conspiracy that sought to suppress, through him, any influence from the East.

Other links would be added to this chain of erudite men: Joseph Görres, in whose Amazonian exuberance myth surfaces like the ruins of a sunken world; K. O. Müller, who died of sunstroke in Greece after having introduced the term "chthonian" into classical studies, as though until then Winckelmann's gods had had no contact with the soil—and even less with the subsoil where Hades reigns: "But Hades and Dionysus are the same god," said Heraclitus. And finally there is the visionary Bachofen, who discovered the most menacing Dionysus of all, the Dionysus who is in league not only with the East but with female sovereignty too.

Until one day—June 18, 1871, to be precise—a young professor at Basle University, one Friedrich Nietzsche, went into the library and borrowed both Creuzer's *Symbolik* and Bachofen's *Gräbersymbolik*. He was close to finishing *The Birth of Tragedy*. Through that book, Dionysus was preparing to burst out onto a stage which now amounted to the whole world.

Only in Nietzsche do the gods reappear with an intensity comparable to that we find in Hölderlin. From *The Birth of Tragedy* to *The Dithyrambs of Dionysus*, and the last "notes of madness," we sense the vibration of something like the same pathos, assuming, that is, that we use the word "pathos" in the way Aristotle meant it, as a technical term which describes what happens in the Mysteries where *"ou matheîn ti deîn, allà patheîn kaì diatethénai"*—"one must not learn but suffer an emotion and be in a certain state."

Unlike their contemporaries, Hölderlin and Nietzsche didn't write *about* the Greeks; rather, from time to time they could themselves become Greeks. The opening of a hymn of Hölderlin's immediately makes one think of certain opening lines in Pindar. In Nietzsche's notebooks we find fragments that might easily be attributed to one of the pre-Socratics, or to Plotinus perhaps—like this one which was written early in 1871: "In man primordial oneness turns towards itself, looking through appearance: appearance reveals essence. Which means: primordial oneness looks at man—to be precise, at the man who is looking at appearance, the man looking through appearance. For man there is *no way toward primordial oneness*. He is all appearance."

Beyond Schopenhauer, this passage gestures toward the ultimate mystery of Eleusis: the double gaze that binds Hades to Kore, the girl who is the pupil, the gaze or look that observes the person looking—and opens up every secret knowledge. Likewise the form of this fragment—all a play on the verb "to look," *schauen*—makes one think more of a Neoplatonist than of a soldier of Bismarck's, which is what Nietzsche had just been, albeit in the role of a nurse.

In those tempestuous days Nietzsche was convinced, as time and again he wrote in his notebooks—that, like tragedy in ancient Greece, myth was about to be reborn "from the spirit of music." Here "music" must be understood as a synonym for Richard Wagner. All one had to do, then, was *recognize it,* since *"in the presence of music we behave as the Greek behaved in the presence of his symbolic myths."* Result: "Thus music has generated myth once again for us." Music was the amniotic fluid needed to protect an obscure process, thanks to which we would once again be able to "feel *mythically*." And here the recurrent dream of the *good* community would lead Nietzsche to make a fatal mistake. Section 23 of *The Birth of Tragedy* is entirely given over to the claim that if *"the gradual reawakening of the Dionysiac spirit* in today's world" was to be magically brought about by Wagner's music, then its true subject would be the "German nature," a euphemism behind which the German *nation* was barely concealed. The reference here is no longer to the Mysteries but to the theatre of European politics, where Germany is being spurred on, albeit with lofty words, to assert its hegemony: "And if the German should look around, hesitant, in search of a guide to lead him back to that long lost homeland, to which he has almost forgotten the path, the road—let him listen to the wonderfully alluring call of the Dionysiac bird, who hovers over him and will show him the way that leads in that direction."

But the ardent decisiveness of these proclamations was complicated, in Nietzsche, by his awareness that the Germany of his time was headed in exactly the opposite direction. While he was writing *The Birth of Tragedy*, sketching out the shape of a civilization that had been radically renewed, Nietzsche was also preparing *The Future of Our Schools*, the most formidable attack ever launched on what is the foundation of the modern conception of culture: education. Nietzsche's premise was that the very institution that ought to represent the culture of the time in its most severe and exemplary form—the illustrious German high school—in fact bore witness to a "growing barbarity in the duties assigned to culture." Behind the progressives' mirage of a "generalized culture," Nietzsche saw only the ferocious determination of the state—and first and foremost the German state—to breed reliable employees. "The factory rules," he noted, summing up the century to come in just a few words. Whenever we claim that culture must *serve some purpose*, he goes on, then sovereignty passes from culture to utility: "You only need to start thinking of culture as something useful and all too soon you'll be confusing what is useful with culture. Generalized culture turns into hatred against true culture." Hence, precisely in its most enlightened and celebrated endeavor, its attempt to bring education to everybody, the modern world was actually guided by a profound aversion to culture. In a fanciful moment immediately after the war with France, Nietzsche had written that perhaps "the Germans had fought the war to free Venus from the Louvre, like a second Helen of Troy." This, he went on, as far as he was concerned, could be the "pneumatic explanation of this war." All the more brutal would be his return to reality a few months later when he heard that the Communards had set fire to the Tuileries. And the Louvre too, insisted the first confused—and, as it turned out, false—reports. Appalled, Nietzsche wrote a letter to Gersdorff over which looms the specter of the "war against civilization." A war waged not, in this instance, by a modern state seeking to make us all slaves to its goals, but by a shapeless multitude, excluded from culture and fundamentally hostile to it, so much so that they sought only to destroy it. Yet Nietzsche couldn't bring himself to condemn the arsonists. He wrote: "It is *we who are guilty* of bringing these horrors to light, all of us, and with our entire past: so we absolutely must not put on pious airs and blame this crime of waging war against civilization on these wretched people alone."

Nietzsche's feelings were divided: on the one hand, he saw European civilization as being on the threshold of a radical regeneration led by Germany; on the other, he saw the modern state in its most advanced form—which is to say the German state—as involved in a systematic project of barbarization, whose first enemy and victim could only be culture itself. But the Germanic infatuation would soon fade. Ahead of Nietzsche lay a life of wandering, a life without a homeland. "Among today's Europeans," he would write, "there are those few who have the right to claim, in the sense of a distinction and an honor, that they are without a homeland." It was to these few that he intended to transmit the *gay science,* a science that would include some of the most precise and ferocious observations ever made *against* Germany, the most vicious being those scattered across the pages of *Ecce Homo*. The only other person who would prove able to wound Germany and German culture so deeply was Gottfried Benn.

The trap Nietzsche had almost fallen into when he was writing *The Birth of Tragedy* was that of fantasizing a future national community behind the variegated surface of the myths: "Knowledge and music allow us to foresee the rebirth of Germany from classical Greece:—it is toward this rebirth that we shall work," he wrote in his notebooks at the time. But his mind was too lucid not to foresee something else as well: "All that is required of us now is that we be slaves of the mass, and in particular slaves of a party." When the sonorous Wagnerian cloud dissolves, even the word "myth" all but disappears from Nietzsche's writing and Dionysus retreats to the wings. But he would be back, with a great clanging of sistra and tambourines: first when he creeps into the voice of that "Dionysiac demon called *Zarathustra,*" and later when from the shadows he maneuvers the enthralling drama that was the last phase of Nietzsche's life. This really did look like an example of a renewed Dionysiac spirit; certainly it was a far cry from the arrogant productive fervor of an imperial Germany. But to be understood, that drama needed a prelude, a sort of summary in shorthand, at once impudent and allusive, of what Nietzsche had come to believe had happened over the course of civilization from the Greeks down to his own time. This is the section "How the 'real world' ended up as a fable" in *Twilight of the Idols*:

1. The real world accessible to the wise man, the pious man, the virtuous man—he lives in it, *he is this world*.

> (The oldest form of the idea, relatively shrewd, simple, persuasive. Transcription of the principle "I, Plato, *am* the truth.")

2. The real world, for the moment inaccessible, but promised to the wise, the pious, the virtuous ("to the sinner who does penance").

> (The idea progresses: grows subtler, more menacing, less easy to grasp—*becomes woman*, becomes Christian . . .)

3. The real world, inaccessible, indemonstrable, unpromissable, but just having thought of it is a consolation, an obligation, a binding imperative.

> (In the background the ancient sun, but seen through a fog of skepticism; the idea become sublime, pale, Nordic, Königsbergian.)

4. The real world—inaccessible? In any event not acceded to. And, in so far as not acceded to,

unknown. Hence, what's more, not a consolation, not a salvation, not binding: what could something unknown bind us to? . . .

> (Gray morning. First yawn of reason. Cock's crow of positivism.)

5. The "real world"—an idea of no use to anyone, and not even binding on us—an idea that has become useless, superfluous, and *consequently* an idea refuted: let's be rid of it!

> (Bright daylight; breakfast time; return of good sense and serenity; Plato blushing for shame; demonic uproar of all free spirits.)

6. We have got rid of the real world: what world is left? the apparent world perhaps? . . . But no! *Along with the real world we've done away with the apparent world as well!*

> (Noon; when the shadows are shortest; end of the longest error of all; zenith of humanity; INCIPIT ZARATHUSTRA.)

This page—which according to an outline drawn up in the spring of 1888 was to be the first of the unfinished *Will to Power*, an opening clash of the cymbals, as it were—should be read together with Hölderlin's prophecies vis-à-vis the "turning back to nativeness." There too we have an attempt to identify the obscure movement that guides history and is such that with the mere passing of time the color of events and the very consistency of the material world is altered. But what a difference in tone! Where Hölderlin is elliptical and solemn, Nietzsche is as brazen as a circus presenter. The jerky rhythm is shot through with an alarming euphoria—and a certain sarcasm too. Yet the process described is grandiose: nothing less than the successive phases of the history of the world, six of them, like the six days of Creation. And it's as though, instead of advancing with dash and confidence, the world were gradually regressing toward its indecipherable origins, a place where, because these categories have yet to split apart, the distinctions "real world" and "apparent world" no longer hold. *Here we are*, announces Nietzsche, and it would be hard not to hear a mocking ring in his voice. We thought we were living in a world where the fog had lifted, a disenchanted, ascertainable, verifiable world. And instead we find that everything has gone back to being a "fable" again. How are we to get our bearings? To which fable should we abandon ourselves, knowing as we do that the next one to come along might overwhelm it? This is the paralysis, the peculiar uncertainty of modern times, a paralysis that all since have experienced. Nietzsche presents it as an ordeal we have to go through: we have been condemned, or elected, to pass through a world without substance, pure specter, where it is true of course that "many new gods are still possible," their feet falling in with a new step, a new dance, "many gods endlessly fleeing each

other, searching out each other, blessedly contradict-
ing each other, many gods hearing each other once
again, once again belonging to each other," yet at the
same time a subtle, indomitable mockery embraces
everything and renders it all uncertain, ephemeral:
parody. It is a frightening development, and Nietzsche
had tried to prepare us for it when, at the end of *The
Gay Science*, he drew the picture of a "spirit who
ingenuously, without wanting to, that is, and out of
an overflowing fullness and strength, begins to play
with everything hitherto considered sacred, good,
untouchable, divine," thus giving rise to the "ideal of
a human-superhuman well-being and kindness, that
may often seem *inhuman*, if set, for example, beside
all the terrestrial seriousness that came before it, or
indeed beside any sort of solemnity of gesture, speech,
expression, gaze, morality, duty, as if this new ideal
were their living and involuntary parody." There it is,
the bow twangs, the word "parody" is let fly—and at
once one senses that this light, reckless, composite,
and sparkling intermezzo serves above all to
announce the moment when once again "the destiny
of the soul is at a turning point, the hand on the clock
face shifts, the tragedy *begins . . .*"

Dazzled by this shiny and deceptive theatre, this
boundless, merry, sinister stage where—the words are
Nietzsche's again—"something extraordinarily nasty
and evil is about to make its debut," because, as we

74

said, *incipit parodia*, we suddenly realize that too many beginnings are going on at the same time. *Incipit tragoedia, incipit parodia, incipit Zarathustra* (inspired by Dionysus). And all at once the answer, the obvious answer, comes to us: they're all the same beginning, at the same moment—and that doesn't just hold for Nietzsche; on the contrary, it sets its seal on the whole world ever since. At this point, what more could Nietzsche do but entrust a last note to the symbolic hands of Jacob Burckhardt? "Actually, I would far rather be a professor at Basle University than God: but I didn't dare push my private selfishness so far as to neglect, just for myself, the creation of the world."

IV

Musings of a Serial Killer

There is a point in the nineteenth century when a secret nadir is reached. It occurs, but without anybody's noticing, when a young man no one has heard of publishes, in Paris and at his own expense, a work entitled *Les Chants de Maldoror*. The year is 1869: Nietzsche is working on *The Birth of Tragedy*; Flaubert publishes *L'Education sentimentale*, Verlaine his *Fêtes galantes*; Rimbaud is writing his first lines. But at the same time something even more drastic is going on: it's as if literature had delegated to the young son of the consulate employee Ducasse, a boy sent to France from Montevideo to complete his studies, the task of carrying out a decisive, clandestine, and violent act. The twenty-three-year-old Isidore assumes the pseudonym Lautréamont, a name probably suggested by a character in the pages of Eugène Sue, and pays an initial deposit of four hundred francs to the publisher Lacroix to have him print his *Chants de Maldoror*. Lacroix takes the money and prints the book—but then refuses to distribute it. As Lautréamont himself would later explain in a letter, Lacroix "refused to have the book appear because it depicted life in such bitter colors that he was afraid of the public prosecutor." But why did *Maldoror* strike such fear into the publisher? Because it was the first book—and that's no exaggeration—written on the principle that *anything and everything* must be the object of sarcasm; not just the century's huge and heavy ballast, an easy target for ridicule, but likewise the work of those who had raged against the ridiculous: Baudelaire, for example, who is irreverently defined as "the morbid lover of the Hottentot Venus," though quite possibly he was Lautréamont's favorite poet, and doubtless his most immediate model. There is no controlling the consequences of such a gesture: it's as though every given—and the whole world is a given—were suddenly kicked off its pedestal to wander about in a dizzying verbal drift where it is submitted to every possible combination and outrage at the hands of an imperturbable juggler: the faceless author Lautréamont, who cancels himself out more completely and more dispassionately than the still somewhat theatrical Rimbaud. To die at twenty-four in a rented room on the rue du Faubourg Montmartre, "sans autres renseignements," as we read in Lautréamont's *acte de décès* is at once a more reckless and effective elimination of identity than to give up writing and become an arms dealer in Africa.

Precisely because the case is so anomalous, it would be wise to approach it through all the customary questions. As, for example: which authors were important to Lautréamont before he published his book? In this regard the young man is helpful, explaining that he spent a great deal of time with "the noxious scribblers: Sand, Balzac, Alexandre Dumas, Musset, Du Terrail, Féval, Flaubert, Baudelaire, Leconte and the *Grève des Forgerons.*" Such a list, however, should be enough in itself to warn us that we are being led into a trap: the inventors of Rocambole and of Madame Bovary are placed on the same level, likewise the popular novelist Féval and Balzac, Baudelaire and François Coppée. It's as though the very idea of there being levels had been discarded. But there is more to be said about influences: in order to unleash Typhoon Maldoror, Lautréamont seems to have taken his cue from a simple observation: that Romantic Satanism had a weak point—it was squeamish. So it won't be enough for the serial killer Maldoror just to rape "the maiden asleep in the plane tree's shade." First he has his bulldog come along with him; then he tells the animal to rip out the girl's throat. But the bulldog "contents himself with just violating in his turn that delicate child's virginity." Annoyed that the creature won't do exactly as he's told, Maldoror takes out "an American pocket knife with ten or twelve blades" and starts rooting about in the maiden's vagina to extract her organs from that "hideous hole." Finally, when her body looks like a "gutted chicken," "he lets the corpse go back to sleep in the plane tree's shade." The evil geniuses of the dark side of Romanticism had usually spared us the details. The writer piled on disturbing adjectives like "unnameable," "monstrous," "perverse," "terrifying," which hardly improved the writing, but at least served to have the monstrous act itself disappear in a soft-focus fade. Lautréamont, on the other hand, takes Satanism at its word. The result is that the reader finds himself seized, as J. Gracq put it, by "the most embarrassing of nervous giggles" until very soon he has no idea at all where he is. In a parody? A clinical manual? Or swept away by a dark poet only a shade more radical than his predecessors?

It's time to take a look at the book's form. The guiding principle behind the writing of *Maldoror* is as follows: take all the literary material that sounds modern—which for the most part at the time we're speaking of meant the Romantic, Satanic, or gothic, depending on who was describing it—then exaggerate it, push it right to the limit, thus draining it of its power, all the while keeping a straight face and making sure to repress a sardonic smile. But Lautréamont went further: quite cold-bloodedly he juxtaposes, or sometimes amalgamates, this feverish and ambitious Satanist literature, which found its greatest exponents in Byron and Baudelaire, with that huge production of inanities and sentimental flourishes that appeared in genre novels for ladies and their maids. So first the horrors of the gothic are described right down to the tiniest detail, rendering them ridiculous, then mixed with the *mièvreries* of the positive and edifying novels of nineteenth-century "social realism," the which are quite implacably reproduced. All conspires to have "tragedy explode in the midst of this frightful frivolity." Everything is reduced to the same level, in the obsessive sound of the same voice, which reaches us "as though amplified by a faulty microphone."

But Lautréamont employs another method too, albeit one that, oddly enough, even his most illustrious critics don't mention, as though it were merely incidental. I'm referring now to his compulsive repetitions: erratic blocks of prose recur, perhaps after only a few lines or a few pages, repeated word for word. They might be single sentences, though of such a kind that one can't help noticing them: "Still a shapeless mass gave dogged chase, following his footsteps in the dust"; or again, "There, in a copse surrounded by flowers, the hermaphrodite, drenched in his tears, has fallen fast asleep on the grass"; or again, "The children chase after her, hurling stones, as if she were a blackbird." In other places the repetition comes with slight variations and is introduced by a sentence that strikes the main chord, as is the case with: "They saw me coming down the valley, while the skin of my breast was still and calm as the slab over a tomb." Or finally, repetitions may multiply and overlap, as in the episode that tells of Falmer, the blond fourteen-year-old with the oval-shaped face whom Maldoror grabs by the hair and "spins around in the air so fast that his scalp was left in his hand while his body shot off with centrifugal force to smash into the trunk of an oak tree . . ."

It's as if the innocuous anaphora, as taught in any textbook of rhetoric, had been blown up beyond all proportion and then set insanely adrift. There are at least two consequences: first, the reading experience is brought close to the essential nature of nightmare, something that lies not so much in the awfulness of the elements that make up a vision, but in the way they keep on and on coming back into the mind. And then the narrative is injected with senselessness, the same way a single word, if repeated often enough, becomes a mere phonic husk freed from any semantic bond.

The premise that lies behind such methods is that the whole world—and in particular every literary form of whatever level—is inevitably cloaked in a poisonous blanket of parody. Nothing is what it claims to be. Everything is already a quotation the moment it appears. This enigmatic and unsettling development, of which few at the time were aware, can be seen as a manifestation of the fact that the whole world, as Nietzsche would soon announce, was going back to being a fable again. Except that now the fable is a heedless whirlwind where the various simulacra are constantly changing places in an egalitarian dust cloud. "Where there are no gods, the phantoms reign," Novalis had prophesied. Now one could go a step further and say: gods and phantoms will alternate on the scene with equal rights. There is no longer a theological power capable of taking charge and putting them in order. In which case, who will risk dealing with them, arranging them? Another power, one that hitherto has been forever denied its independence, forever obliged to serve society, but which now threatens to hoist anchor for good and set sail, sovereign and solitary, as the vessel that brings together all the simulacra and wanders about the ocean of the mind for the pure pleasure and play of the gesture: literature. Which in this mutation may also be called absolute literature.

That parody is the governing principle behind all Lautréamont's work is not easily demonstrated. For strictly speaking with Lautréamont *nothing* can be demonstrated. With great discipline he left not a single sentence—not even in his letters—that we might with any confidence *take seriously*. In vain does one look for some sort of declaration of his poetics, unless that poetics resides precisely in the suspicion that every word he wrote is a spoof. It's a suspicion that will become overwhelming when we turn to look at the second phase of his work: the slim collection entitled

Poésies. And even more so if we hear how he spoke of the book before it appeared. In October 1869 Lautréamont wrote to Poulet-Malassis: "I have celebrated evil as did Mickiewicz, Byron, Milton, Southey, A. de Musset, Baudelaire, etc. Of course I exaggerated the pitch a bit to do something new along the lines of that sublime literature that celebrates desperation only so as to oppress the reader and have him desire the good as a remedy." These lines themselves are sharp with the bracing air of mockery. But here we must reconstruct what they leave implicit: the *Chants de Maldoror* were at that time languishing in printed sheets stacked in the warehouse of a publisher tormented by the prospect of prosecution. At first, according to Lacroix, Lautréamont "refused to amend the violence of his text." He still hadn't paid Lacroix an outstanding balance of 800 francs for the print run, and refused to do so unless the book was distributed. The situation was deadlocked, something that was in the interests of neither author nor printer. It was thus that they turned to Poulet-Malassis, a bibliophile and publisher experienced in finding the right channels for unloading risky books. Eager to come to an agreement, Lautréamont writes to Poulet-Malassis, "Sell them, I won't stop you: what do I have to do in return? Dictate your terms," and at the same time, to suggest how he might launch the book, he resorts to the ludicrous idea of the writer who celebrates evil to "oppress the reader" and thus have him turn to the good. Oddly, the publisher accepts the suggestion. Only two days later, in the *Bulletin trimestriel des publications défendues en France imprimées à l'étranger,* a publication Poulet-Malassis used to announce his new titles, Lautréamont's book is presented thus:

"There are no more Manichaeans," Pangloss used to say. "There is me," Martin would answer. The author of this book belongs to a species no less rare. Like Baudelaire, like Flaubert, he believes that the aesthetic expression of evil implies the keenest appetite for the good, the highest possible morality.

Poulet-Malassis was far more perceptive and worldly-wise than Lacroix, whom Baudelaire loathed. So the same mockery implicit in Lautréamont's letter—was he thinking, when he spoke of having "exaggerated the pitch a bit" at least as far as the erotic was concerned (for that was the area Poulet-Malassis specialized in), of the description of "long, chaste, and dreadful" sex between Maldoror and an "enormous female shark," a coupling that would one day delight Huysmans?—that same mockery is now echoed in the publicity for the book. It's as if in writing to his new distributor Lautréamont had given him instructions on how to camouflage the book so that it could be introduced into the world. Yet, at the end of the same letter, we hear a different tone creeping in. Having begged Poulet-Malassis to send the book to the most important reviewers, Lautréamont adds: "They alone will pass judgment in first and last instance on the beginning of a publication that will see its end of course only later when I myself have seen mine. That's why the moral at the end isn't there yet. But there is immense pain on every page. Is that evil?" The final, piercing question is one of those rare flickers where Lautréamont seems to speak to us *directly*, without the mediation of the outrageous and mocking. But it's worth noticing another detail: he refers to *Maldoror* as a sort of *carmen perpetuum* that will be over only when the author himself is dead. Before then we can't know what "the moral at the end" will be. Implication: perhaps "the good" the text is supposed to prompt us toward is also a temporary conclusion, to be turned on its head at will. And this is another of those hints that light up *Maldoror* like a phantasmagoria teeming with snares and pitfalls.

Four months after the first letter to Poulet-Malassis, on February 21st, 1870, Lautréamont writes another. It seems there has been no progress: "Has Lacroix handed over the edition or done anything else with it? Or have you rejected it? He hasn't told me anything. I haven't seen him since." But during those months Lautréamont's lucubration had taken him a decisive step forward. As he immediately goes on to announce:

> You should know that I have repudiated my past. These days I celebrate only hope; but in order to do that I must first of all attack the century's doubt (melancholies, sadnesses, griefs, desperations, lugubrious whinnyings, sham nastinesses, infantile prides, laughable calamities, etc., etc.). In early March I will be giving Lacroix a book where I take the finest poems of Lamartine, Victor Hugo, Alfred de Musset, Byron, and Baudelaire, and correct them so that they celebrate hope; I show how they should have been written. At the same time I correct six of the worst passages of my accursed book.

This is how he presents the *Poésies*. In those four months, then, Lautréamont seems to have realized that in order to introduce his monstrous *Maldoror* into the world, it wouldn't be enough to claim he was celebrating evil to turn people to the good, an argument dangerously similar to that of pornographers who claim they are operating in defense of chastity. So why not celebrate the good directly? Thus a new method of working takes shape, one that is even more offensive and pernicious than that used in creating Maldoror, one, you might even say, that raises monstrosity exponentially to the power of two: he will correct other people's writings "in order that they celebrate hope." The premise now is that every boundary between literary properties has been pulled down. Authors are stooges. Literature is a continuum of words to be interfered with as one pleases, by transforming every sign into its opposite, if that's what we want. But having set out along the path of total mockery, Lautréamont can't stop himself, even if he wants to. What has been squared may just as well be cubed. So, why restrict oneself to correcting authors celebrating evil by turning their work round toward the good? Why not correct the authors who represent the good? And who would they be? By definition, the authors you read in school.

Again, this higher level of exasperation, which now sweeps all before it, Good and Bad alike, is announced in a letter, a letter that was to be Lautréamont's last. This time it is addressed to the family banker, Darasse, who was sending the young man a monthly pittance. Lautréamont writes to ask for an advance so as to be able to pay for the printing of a book that this time is impeccably virtuous. After a brief account of his troubles with Lacroix, he adds:

> The whole thing was pointless. It has opened my eyes. I said to myself that, since the poetry of doubt (of the books of today no more than a hundred and fifty pages will survive) has reached a point of such

dark desperation and theoretical iniquity, it follows that it is radically false; for this reason, *they put principles in doubt, principles that must be placed beyond discussion*: it is worse than wicked. The poetic groanings of this century are no more than hideous sophisms. To celebrate tedium, grief, sadness, melancholy, death, darkness, obscurity, etc., means to insist on looking only and willy-nilly at the infantile reverse of everything. Lamartine, Hugo, Musset, they have all voluntarily metamorphosed into milksops. They are the Great Soft Heads of our age. Always sniveling! That's why I've completely changed my methods, so as to celebrate nothing but *hope*, TRANQUILITY, *happiness*, DUTY. That way I can re-establish my links with the Corneilles and Racines along that chain of good sense and sangfroid that was brusquely interrupted by those poseurs Voltaire and Rousseau.

It's worth noting a few details. First, this letter wasn't written to a publisher, like Poulet-Malassis, who had been a friend of Baudelaire's, but to a banker, who tended to treat his client's young son with a "deplorable and systematic diffidence" entirely in line with his job. What's more, given its nature, the letter seemed destined to be lost along with countless others of the same variety. In fact, it owes its survival only to a chance encounter laden with Ducassian irony: in 1978 an electrician from Gavray, not far from the English Channel, found it in a pile of old papers on sale at a junk dealer's in Porbail near Valognes.

Writing to Darasse, Lautréamont assumes the petitioning tone of him who, while asking for an advance of cash, is eager to reassure the family banker by coming across as a young fellow of good morals. Yet at the same time the banker becomes his guinea pig, because many of the expressions used in the letter can be found almost word for word in the *Poésies*. Thus Lautréamont achieves a sort of white heat of mockery—while once again displaying that peculiarity, a congenital defect almost, that Artaud would describe thus: "[Lautréamont] can't write a simple, ordinary letter without our sensing an epileptic tremor of the Word so that, whatever is being discussed, it refuses to be used without a shudder." But what will happen if that "epileptic tremor of the Word" is put at the service, as Lautréamont now claims, of that "famous idea of the good" cultivated by "teaching staffs and preservers of the just" who direct "generations young and old along the path of honesty and hard work"?

The result will be *Poésies*, a work that appeared in two installments distinguished by Roman numerals: as of today there are two remaining copies of *Poésies I;* only one, in the Bibliothèque Nationale in Paris, of *Poésies II.* This too must be added to the long list of Lautréamont's glorious firsts. Though in these books he went back to using his real name: Isidore Ducasse. Why hide, after all, when this work, as he claimed, can "be read by a fourteen-year-old girl"?

Poésies I offers a drastic declaration of intent that solemnly resumes and expands the ideas set out in the letter to the banker Darasse. All the same, one soon encounters a first, brutal breach of the rules of belles lettres: a paragraph a page and a half long made up of a single sentence where the main verb appears after forty-eight lines at the end of an *enumeración caotica* of the elements that constitute the literature he is condemning. To our eyes today the paragraph presents itself as a superb parody of *all* nineteenth-century literature. It opens with "the perturbances, the anxieties, the depravations"; the list then proceeds for twenty or so lines with "the damp-hen smells, the languors, the frogs, the cuttlefish, the sharks, the desert simoom, all that is somnambulistic, sinister, nocturnal, somniferous, night-wandering, sticky, seal-speaking, ambiguous, consumptive, spasmodic, aphrodisiac, anemic, one-eyed"—and so it goes on with a momentum all its own, until finally the author declares all the elements in his list "filthy flesh heaps I blush to mention." This having mentioned exactly one hundred and one of them, blushing no doubt with every new entry. And on the subject of "flesh heaps," the reader of *Maldoror* will at once connect them to the ghostly Mervyn when he speaks of the "place where my glacial immobility resides, surrounded by a long row of empty rooms, filthy flesh heaps of my hours of boredom."

But Lautréamont doesn't let us dwell on such things, and only a few lines after that extraordinarily long list he is already announcing a new literary canon: "The masterpieces of the French language are school prize-giving speeches and academic disquisitions." And now it's as if Lautréamont were already looking forward to an unprecedented pleasure: not, as in *Maldoror*, setting the lushness of monstrosity against an obtuse and upright order, but drawing instead on the monstrosity already present within the order itself, and this simply by using the technique most congenial to him—that of taking things literally and pushing them to their furthest extremes. All too soon he is soaring to the following conclusion: "Any literature that challenges the eternal truths is condemned to feed only on itself. It is wrong. It devours its own liver. The *novissima verba* raise a superb smile on the faces of the snotty brats at school. We have no right to question the Creator about anything." Still savoring these peremptory and vacuous announcements, we may well be struck by the following thought: that what we are reading is itself one of the purest examples of a *literature that feeds only on itself*.

But let's move on now to *Poésies II*: for here the perverse mechanism heralded in *Poésies I* is immediately set in action. The method now is plagiarism—or, to be precise, plagiarism with inversion and a reversal of terms. It works like this: you take passages from the great classics (the favorites are first Pascal, who dominates, then La Rochefoucauld, Vauvenargues, and La Bruyère, but there is still space for a couple of moderns like Hugo and Vigny), and you present as affirmation what was in fact negation, or, of course, vice versa. The inversion technique creates various effects. The most frequent is a tendency to neutralize, to render meaningless both the inverted passage and the shadow passage behind it, often something extremely well known. To this end, Lautréamont's most effective device is his elimination of the empty space between one passage and the next, something that forces each aphoristic splinter or denser fragment to accept its position in a calm and impassive sequence of non sequiturs. On other occasions, however, inversion sparks off something quite different: a fierce flash that illuminates the malign torturer of texts more than the classical text tortured. Here is an example from a piece by Pascal on happiness, a piece that ends in an oddly edifying tone, deploring the man "who seeks for it in vain in external things and is forever dissatisfied since happiness is neither in us nor in creation, but in God alone." Thus Pascal, but it could be any one of countless spiritual advisers passing a proverbial and very French buck to each other across the centuries.

Until along comes Lautréamont and we have this: "Man gets bored, he seeks this multitude of occupations. He has the idea of the happiness he has conquered: finding it in himself, he looks for it in external things. He is satisfied. Unhappiness is neither in us nor in the creatures. It is in Elohim." In the last sentence, and quite unexpectedly, the mocking joke is elevated to the level of Gnostic pronouncement. But the process doesn't end here. A little further on, taking as his shadow text a pompous passage from Vauvenargues, full of exclamation marks and rhetorical questions, Lautréamont drains it of bombast and restores it to sobriety while once again altering its meaning, this time toward a grim scenario of cosmic struggle: "We know what the sun and the heavens are. We possess the secrets of their movements. In the hand of Elohim, blind instrument, unfeeling mechanism, the world attracts our homage. The revolutions of empires, the aspects of the times, the nations, the conquerors of science, all of this springs from an atom that creeps up, lasts but a day, destroys the spectacle of the universe, in every age." Lautréamont's voice rings out unmistakable in that "destroys the spectacle of the universe"; the corresponding words in Vauvenargues read: "embraces somehow in a single glance the spectacle of the universe in every age." But perhaps the final outrage comes a few lines later (and immediately before the end), where the shadow text now is a famous passage from La Bruyère that runs thus: "Everything has been said, and we come too late after seven thousand years of men thinking before us. As far as customs are concerned, the beautiful and the best have already been taken. We but glean a field already harvested by the ancients and the more able of the modern." Watch out for the inversions in Lautréamont: "Nothing has been said. We come too soon after seven thousand years of men. As far as customs are concerned, *and the rest too for that matter* [I emphasize the words not there in La Bruyère], the worst has already been taken. We have the advantage of coming after the ancients, we able among the moderns." La Bruyère's words are the very *exemplum* of culture, of the slow transmission of knowledge, of that *douceur* that over time seeps into civilization, smoothes its rough edges, saps its harsh energy. Lautréamont's words are the pronouncement of the artificial barbarian as he prepares to escape from aphasia, though it is still "too soon." And the whole of the past is dismissed with contempt as no more than a servile chain of men transmitting a knowledge that regards "the worst part" of everything. But then, as *Poésies II* had already pronounced earlier on, inverting Vauvenargues: "One can be just, if one is not human."

We reach the end of *Poésies II* infected at once by an insane hilarity and by a vast sense of unease. It's a response we haven't experienced in relation to any other piece of literature, but very like the sensation of aphasia Max Stirner evokes at the end of *The Unique*. One might say that Stirner and Lautréamont have in common something none of their contemporaries share: it is the lethal dagger-point of a personal autonomy that presents itself as a quietly autistic delirium. Thus Maldoror ponders: "If I exist, I am not another. I cannot accept this ambiguous plurality in myself. I want to be alone in my inner reasoning. Autonomy . . . or if not may I be turned into a hippopotamus." Here the infinitesimal splinter of the individual subject opposes itself, exactly as in Stirner's *The Unique*, to any and every *other*, but above all to that devastating Other in whom it is not hard to recognize the "Celestial Bandit," the fatal Demiurge, always ready to creep in everywhere—and above all into the nooks and crannies of the individual's mental life—with his "ferocious curiosity." Because this is the point, Maldoror goes on: "My subjectivity and the Creator are too much for the one brain." As Remy de Gourmont would one day so concisely remark: "[Lautréamont] sees no one else in the world but himself and God—and God bothers him."

After Stirner, Lautréamont is the second artificial barbarian to burst onto the scene. Not this time a barbarian of the spirit, but of literature. Just as Stirner had shown the rash neo-Hegelians that they were a band of bigots, in awe of the state and humanity, so, painstakingly, patiently, clear-sightedly, Lautréamont shows the Romantic Satanists, a huge tribe that culminated in Baudelaire, that they had no more than nibbled the first fruits of gothic horror; they hadn't gone into the details. Even the places that it is reasonable to suppose produced these poisonous clouds were similar: rented rooms in big cities, Berlin or Paris, upper floors, the sky deep behind the windows, shadows on the walls. In both men's pasts there are hints of an overheated, fanciful, frenzied adolescence that "thrived on the violation of duty," imprisoned between college walls that "breed in their thousands the scalding, unappeasable resentments that can brand a whole life with their fire."

A suppressed and destructive fury, a magmatic form. Léon Bloy, the first reader equal to Lautréamont, sensed it at once: "It is liquid lava. Something wild, black, devouring." Only of Lautréamont and Stirner do we have no portraits (of Stirner there is a profile with glasses, sketched by Engels on a tavern menu). Stirner treats the philosophy that came before him (the most audacious philosophy) the way Lautréamont treats the literature of the Romantic rebels: pushing it to the limit to destroy it. Both were inspired by a blasphemous craving to see what would happen if they poured scorn on absolutely all the rules. Next to nothing, of course, is the answer, in the sense that hardly anyone realized what they were up to. But the gesture remains. After them every philosophy and every literature would be shot through by a fatal flaw.

V

An Abandoned Room

The principal argument leveled against the Greek myths was always of a moral, and above all a sexual, nature: the myths, it appeared, were to be condemned because full of unseemly stories, the chief offenders being the gods themselves. The objection was not, as some might suppose, invented by the Church Fathers; all they did, duty bound as they were, was to pad it out. We can find it in Xenophanes or, in exemplary form, in Plato. After which every age would color it as they chose, from the Alexandrians through to the Rococo. Indeed, the long chain of condemnation had still to be broken when, in 1879, Stéphane Mallarmé set out to translate and adapt a handbook of mythology: the Reverend George W. Cox's *Manual of Mythology*. Mallarmé had taken on the job—the book was to be used in secondary schools—partly because he needed the money, but partly too out of the same privately esoteric propensities that a few years before had prompted him to produce and edit every word of a frivolous magazine called *La Dernière Mode*, a publication that could still, he claimed, when pulled out and dusted off, make him "dream for hours." In adapting Cox's text to the "French spirit," Mallarmé made cuts and additions, paraphrasing here and reformulating there. The criteria he applied are revealing, so much so that when we come across a difference between the two texts, we immediately find ourselves wondering how and why Mallarmé made his changes. Until at a certain point the eye falls on a quite remarkable statement: "Si les dieux ne font rien d'inconvenant, c'est alors qu'ils ne sont plus dieux du tout"—"If the gods do nothing unseemly, then they are no longer gods at all."

Twenty-five centuries of morality—pagan, Christian, and secular—seem to fall away before these words. Can it be, then, that in order to be a god one *must* be involved in unseemly behavior? Can it be that that vast repertoire of unnameable acts we come across in the ancient fables is itself the code through which the gods make themselves manifest? Such a theological vision would demand long and considered reflection. And in the end it might actually turn out to be more farsighted than the usual disapproval, at least if we think of it as the unsettling prelude to some kind of mystery. Having recovered from the shock, we turn at once to check Cox's text, where we discover that the Reverend was himself translating, correctly this time, from Euripides: "If the gods do aught unseemly, then they are not gods at all." Which is the opposite of what Mallarmé wrote. Yet his translation of the surrounding context respects Cox's work in every detail, a state of affairs that prompted Bertrand Marchal to offer the following hypothesis: "It is nevertheless possible that Mallarmé did in fact write 'Si les dieux font rien d'inconvenant,' and that an overzealous typesetter added the regrettable *ne*, which the poet then failed to pick up." Theological catastrophe thus comes, in this version of events, as the consequence of the fussiness of the setter and a mental lapse on the part of the poet. After long years of persecution, the revenge of the pagan gods, we are invited to suppose, reaches its acme in a misprint, something all the more significant in that it occurs on a page written by the very man who said he wanted to eliminate chance from writing. If this were the case, we should have to confess that no one before then had dared even conceive of the idea that chance, on this occasion, helped to formulate.

But the whole thing will take on a different light if we recall Lautréamont's *Poésies*: for Mallarmé's scandalous statement looks very like something Lautréamont might have come up with using his sarcastic process of plagiarism plus inversion. At which point it's as if the uncertainty, indeed vertigo, that *Poésies* inspires had spread, stretching out silky octopus tentacles as far as Mallarmé; as if this huge joke at literature's expense were now mingling its lymph with the work of a man who attempted the supreme vindication of literature.

That sentence about the gods reminds us of another curiosity in Mallarmé's adaptation of Cox, one that cannot this time be attributed to the mischievous vagaries of chance. Almost every time Cox writes "God," Mallarmé translates the word as "divinity." And the moment of "maximum deviation" comes *in the paragraph immediately after* the scandalous statement above, as follows:

COX: "Zeus was a mere name by which they might speak of Him in whom we live and move, and have our being."

MALLARMÉ: *"Zeus était un pur nom, à la faveur de quoi il leur fût possible de parler de la divinité, inscrite au fond de notre être."*

The deviation is evident and the consequences far-reaching. On the one hand we have Cox, who treats the Greeks as children allowed only a confused glimpse of that truth which will only become available through the Christian revelation, the appearance of Him *who* truly is that *Person* "in whom we live and move and have our being," as the King James Version so eloquently translates Saint Paul's words to the Athenians. On the other we have Mallarmé, who refers to an impersonal entity of which he says only, in words both sober and mysterious, that it is "inscribed in the very ground of our being." But what did Mallarmé mean when he used the word "divinity"? Rather than to the gods, who in their Parnassian version could all too easily be suspected of heralding some noble kind of rhythmic gymnastics, or at best looking forward to Isadora Duncan, Mallarmé was always drawn to a neutral form of the divine, an underlying ground beneath everything else, nourishing everything else and from which all else springs, a ground at once cosmic and mental, equally shared out, and of which he would one day write: "There must be something occult in the ground of everyone; I firmly believe in something hidden away, a closed and secret signifier, that inhabits the ordinary." But before gaining access to that "closed and secret signifier," which was to be his entire opus, Mallarmé was to go through a ferocious, silent, and protracted mental drama that culminated in a "terrible struggle with that old and evil plumage, happily brought to earth, God." To be more precise: "That struggle took place on his bony wing, the which, in more vigorous death throes than I had thought possible from him, had dragged me into the Shadows." The first thing we can say about this duel is that it takes place just months before the gruesome descriptions of repeated battles between Maldoror and his Creator, as for example when the latter sees "the annals of the heavens knocked off their pedestal," while Maldoror applies his "four hundred suckers to the hollow of his armpit," causing him to "let out terrible screams."

Before approaching any underlying divine ground, then, one first had to kill a being called God, an old and tenacious bird who clung to his antagonist throughout long-protracted death throes. And what would happen when the fight was over? Again, in a letter from the same period, Mallarmé recounts: "I had just drawn up the plan of my entire life's work, having found the key to myself—the keystone, or center, if you like, so as not to mix ourselves up with metaphor, the center of myself, where I dwell like a sacred spider, on the principal threads already spun from my mind, and with the help of which I will weave, *at the crossing points*, some marvelous laces, which I can foresee and which already exist in the bosom of Beauty." Like the "bony wing," this "sacred spider" also belongs to the zoology of Lautréamont. What went on in the secret depths of the mind seemed anxiously to be awaiting this new teratologist, the visionary who would expand the animal realm to include new kinds of monsters.

But why does Mallarmé call himself a "sacred" spider? Is it that, having brought down the old plumage, God, he plans, in a delirium of omnipotence, to take his place? Or was it rather a delirium of impotence that afflicted the young English teacher, secluded as he was in the gloomiest of provinces? Neither one nor the other. In referring to himself as a "sacred spider,"

Mallarmé was doing no more, no less, than performing his function as a poet, which is first of all that of being precise. What he couldn't know was that he wasn't speaking of himself, but of the Self, the *ātman*.

Let us open the *Bṛhadāraṇyaka Upaniṣad*:

"As a spider sends forth its thread, as small sparks rise from the fire, so all senses, all worlds, all gods, all beings, spring from the Self."

And another Upaniṣad speaks of a "single god who like a spider cloaks himself in the threads spun from the primordial matter [*pradhāna*], according to his nature [*svabhāvataḥ*]." And another again says: "As a spider spins out and swallows up his thread, as the grasses spring from the earth, as the hairs from the head and body of a living being, so everything here springs from the indestructible."

Unfamiliar with the Vedic texts, barely initiated in the rudiments of Buddhism by his friend Lefébure and always punctilious in rejecting any direct connection with it ("the Nothing, which I arrived at without knowing Buddhism," he says), Mallarmé was clearing a path toward something that had no name in the lexicon of his times, but within which he would always live and work. It was the same thing to which three years later he planned to dedicate a *thèse d'agrégation*, of which only the title now remains: *De divinitate*. But we do know that Mallarmé saw in that thesis both the outcome and the convalescence of a long, devastating process that had transformed him into another being.

The acute, precipitous phase of that process lasted a year, from May 1866 to May 1867. Mallarmé was then a twenty-four-year-old English teacher at the high school in Tournon, moving later to Besançon, where the climate is "black, damp, and icy." He came from a family who had long been and still were Public Registry officials. In his family, to "have a career" meant to have a career in the Registry Office. Mallarmé was the first to betray his breed, choosing poetry. Already he had sensed that the world around him had "a kitchen smell." As a poet, his main task would be to work Baudelaire's furrow and push it that little bit further. This he had already started to do, with great mastery, when he wrote "L'Azur" and "Brise marine." Then, in the spring of 1866, Mallarmé spends a week in Cannes and *something happens*—a sort of primordial event that looks forward to Valéry's "night in Genoa." His first mention of it comes in a letter to Cazalis on April 28th.

Mallarmé explains: "Quarrying the verse to that point I encountered two chasms, which bring me to despair. One is Nothingness." This "crushing thought" forced him to abandon writing poetry. But immediately afterwards Mallarmé launches into a paragraph that lays a sort of metaphysical foundation for the poetry he was yet to write: "Yes, *I know*, we are nothing but vain forms of matter—yet sublime too when you think that we invented God and our own souls. So sublime, my friend! that I want to give myself this spectacle of a matter aware, yes, of what it is but throwing itself madly into the Dream that it knows it is not, singing the Soul and all those divine impressions that gather in us from earliest childhood, and proclaiming, before the Nothingness that is the truth, those glorious falsehoods!" The threads that interweave in this sentence would go on spinning out until Mallarmé's death. And likewise the ambiguities: above all in that verb *s'élançant* ("throwing itself"), in which converge both the subject who wants to give himself "this spectacle of a matter," etc., and the matter itself observing its own behavior.

At this point we realize we have been abruptly introduced into that geometrical locus called Mallarmé. Immediately the atmosphere is both chemical—a vivisection laboratory, in fact—and alchemical: the heat of the *opus alchymicum*. This, then, is the great atmosphere of *décadence*, something that sprang before anything else out of a dissociation of forms and psyche. Mallarmé was to become at once the high priest and the scientist of this process, which, in fact, was already at work. In July Mallarmé observes, once again for the benefit of Cazalis: "For a month now I have been in the pure glaciers of aesthetics—having discovered Nothingness I have found the Beautiful." And the work starts to take shape, not *une oeuvre* now, but "*le Grand Oeuvre,* as our forebears the alchemists used to say." A long period of elaboration would be required: "I shall give myself twenty years to bring it [the opus] to completion, and the rest of my life will be given over to an Aesthetics of Poetry."

What was going on? "A descent into Nothingness," which we could liken to a *saison en enfer,* but not of the torrid and turbulent variety Rimbaud experienced. On the contrary, from the outside there was nothing to be seen: like a building that dissolves into rubble and dust while the façade remains intact—until one day the windows are empty sockets framing the sky *behind* them. Something chilling and secretive was happening. Mallarmé describes it thus: "I really have decomposed, and to think that this is what it takes to have a vision of the universe that is really whole! Otherwise, the only wholeness one feels is that of one's own life. In a museum in London there is an exhibit called 'The Value of a Man': a long coffinlike box with lots of compartments where they've put starch—phosphorus—flour—bottles of water and alcohol—and big pieces of gelatin. I am a man like that." Once again we sense the all-pervasive, slightly nauseous smell of formaldehyde. But who is it describing himself in this way? The obscure English teacher—or someone else? Or who in him?

So it is that once again the Progenitor, the Prajāpati of the Brāhmaṇas, appears on the scene: exhausted, dislocated, breath rattling in his throat, it is he who had to decompose before anything else could appear and exist. Including the gods, for they too are beings with a shape and hence do not know the spasm of the "indefinite," *anirukta*, from which they sprang and which glows within them. But this time, shrugging off the fog of centuries, Prajāpati finds himself transposed into the golden age of positivism, when man is no more than physics plus chemistry, and consciousness but a vague by-product of the higher functions, something nobody has time to be bothered with. This too the Progenitor would have to put up with, one more insult in his interminably long life. But why had Mallarmé gone looking for Prajāpati, without even knowing who he was?

Here modern and primordial meet and a spark is struck: to create a work of absolute literature one must reunite oneself with the indistinct time before the gods were born, the time when Prajāpati elaborated, with that "ardor" or heat that is called *tapas*, his desire for an outward existence that would be both visible and palpable. When Mallarmé spoke of the fire beneath his alchemist's crucible, he was referring to that same *tapas*. And in fact he had always felt drawn to this obscure figure, always been ready to be led that way, ready to have the elements of his body deposit out into those gloomy chemical compartments that remind us at once of pharmacy and of morgue. But who did the leading? The poet answers: "Destruction was my Beatrice."

In Mallarmé's apartment there was a Venetian mirror, a talisman. During the process that had "dragged" him down "into the Shadows," he felt he was sinking "desperately and infinitely" into that mirror. For now it no longer reflected the poet looking into it and studying his reflection there. But one day Mallarmé would surface in the mirror again, like a piece of flotsam in a pond. He looked at himself, recognized himself—and went back to his old life. But he knew that something had changed—and his closest friend, Cazalis, sensed it too: he was no longer, Mallarmé wrote to him, the "Stéphane you knew—but a disposition of the Spiritual Universe to see itself and develop itself, through what I was." These words, which in a newsy letter to a friend sound, as it were, calmly delirious, will seem perfectly plausible and even self-evident if we think of them as a description of an episode in the life of Prajāpati. Mallarmé was trying to give a name to a process that had *not been recorded* in the lexicon of the tradition he worked in. Yet he kept trying, as if with a presentiment that that impossible path was the only one available to him. But what was the link that welded Mallarmé to that being, Prajāpati, of whom the West knew absolutely nothing then (not one of the Brāhmaṇas had been translated at the time)?

A word: *manas*, "mind" (the Latin *mens*). The Brāhmaṇas say: "Prajāpati is, so to speak, the mind," or elsewhere, "The mind is Prajāpati." If we had to define that characteristic which makes Mallarmé so radically different from the poetry that came before—and after—we would have to say: never had poetry been so magnificently superimposed upon the most elementary and mysterious fact of all—that a certain fragment of matter is endowed with that quality which is like no other, that is, on the contrary, the very *medium* in which every quality and every likeness appear, and which is called "consciousness."

As Proust would one day write to Reynaldo Hahn, it is not true that in Mallarmé images disappear. No, they are "still images of things, since we would never be able to imagine anything else, only that they are reflected, as it were, in a smooth dark mirror of black marble." And that "black marble" is the mind. In Mallarmé the material of poetry is brought back, with unprecedented and as yet unrepeated determination, to mental experience. Shut away in an invisible *templum*, the word evokes, one after another, simulacra, mutations, events, all of which issue and disperse in the sealed chamber of the mind, where the primordial crucible burns. This is the place the reader is invited to discover, but before he can penetrate it he will have to make the same journey the poet did. This is what Mallarmé meant when he insisted so stubbornly that his poetry was composed of effects and suggestions that must act as if on a mental keyboard. Never state the thing, but the resonance of the thing. Why this obsession? Many recent readers have taken this precept of Mallarmé's to imply a reduction of the world to the word, with the inevitable consequence that all becomes entirely self-referential and self-sufficient. But this is not the case: on the contrary, such a vision impoverishes and frustrates what is secretly at work in this poetry. The premise behind this interpretation is one that governs much of our world today—indeed, that makes it possible for that world to operate—but that at the same time leaves it unable to grasp a great deal of what is essential. In its most concise form this premise declares that thought is language. More ambitiously it claims that the mind is language. But we do not think in words. Or rather, we *sometimes* think in words. Words are scattered archipelagos, drifting, sporadic. The mind is the sea. To recognize this sea in the mind seems to have become something forbidden, something that the presiding orthodoxies, in their various manifestations, whether scientist or merely commonsensical, instinctively avoid. Yet this is the crucial parting of the ways. It is at this crossroads that we decide in which direction knowledge will go.

A question presents itself: in what way, then, did the tremendous upheaval Mallarmé experienced between May 1866 and May 1867 manifest itself in his poetry? Let's look at the sonnet that is known as "in *ix*," because it includes a sequence of difficult rhymes in *ix*. The poem is defined by Mallarmé as "a sonnet allegorical of itself," and this definition immediately serves as a warning that we are on the threshold of something that had never been tried before. In an age where allegory was becoming no more than an appendage of the department of public works, used mainly in the conception of those clumsily complacent monuments that celebrate some capitalized abstraction, as, for example, Humanity, Country, Progress, Victory, or whatever—in such an age merely to claim that a sequence of words was offering something "allegorical of itself" was a gesture of impertinent defiance. Equally challenging was the decision to build the sonnet around rhymes in *ix*—rhymes among the rarest in the French language, so much so that while working on the poem Mallarmé had to ask his friends if anyone knew the exact meaning of the word *ptyx*, which he needed for a rhyme. But though this may be the most immediately noticeable aspect of the poem, it is not the most important.

The territory that this sonnet sets out to conquer is

certainly not that of the virtuoso sequence of *ix* rhymes. The poets of the Baroque, after all, had produced any number of such feats, and a trip to the library would have more than satisfied anyone's desires for that kind of thing. Nor is it the play of refractions, the "mirage within the words themselves," to use the precept that Mallarmé explained thus: "I believe that . . . what we should be aiming for above all in poetry is to have the words reflect each other to the point that they no longer retain their own color but can only be seen as transitions in a spectrum." This rule would apply to all Mallarmé's poetry: but to understand it we must first establish *the space* within which the rule operates.

To help us approach that space, we have at our disposal—and it's a rare privilege indeed—a paraphrase of this least paraphrasable of sonnets, written by the author himself. Mallarmé wrote it because the sonnet was to be included in a collection of poems by various authors, each poem being printed beside an etching. He wanted his illustration to be "full of Dream and Emptiness"; and to help the eventual artist, who in fact never materialized, because the poem was rejected, no doubt because considered incomprehensible, Mallarmé paraphrased his poem thus:

For example, an open window at night, the two shutters secured; a room with no one in it, despite the stable atmosphere produced by the secured shutters, and in a night made of absence and questioning, no furniture, except perhaps some plausible hint of vague *consoles*, a frame, combative, with death throes, around a mirror hung in the background, with its reflection, starry and incomprehensible, of the Ursa Major, the Great Bear, that connects this abandoned lodging of the world to the sky alone.

This paraphrase, itself an enchanted shred of prose, refers to the one lyric of which Mallarmé declared that he didn't even know if it made sense or not, and that even if it didn't the author nevertheless "would take comfort from it . . . thanks to the amount of poetry that it contains." All of which will serve as the definitive demonstration that the only acceptable paraphrase is not the one that results from the improvident determination to translate a poem into some supposed meaning, but on the contrary *a literary genre in its own right*. And one that in this case is especially precious to us, because it states the implicit subject of the poem: the "room with no one in it." It has been observed that from the upheaval of 1866 on, Mallarmé's poetry abandons the outside world and shuts itself away in a room. But what is this room that coincides with the very space of the poem? Could it be that room "with no one in it," inhabited only by a mirror?

And who was it who just left that room, a few seconds, or millennia, ago?

There is a very strong and very ancient emotion that is rarely mentioned or recognized: it is the anguish we feel for the absence of idols. If the eye has no image on which to rest, if there is nothing to mediate between the mental phantasm and that which simply is, then a subtle despondency creeps in. This is the atmosphere that reigns in the first dream of which we have a record, a dream told by a woman, Addudûri, overseer of the palace of Mari in Mesopotamia, in a letter etched on clay tablets more than three thousand years ago. "In my dream I had gone into the temple of the goddess Bêllit-ekallim; but the statue of Bêllit-ekallim wasn't there! Nor were the statues of the other divinities that normally stand beside Her. Faced with this sight I wept and wept." The first of all dreams speaks of an empty temple, like Mallarmé's empty room. The statues have been carried off, deported perhaps, along with the people who worshiped them. That kind of thing happened then. Loss precedes presence: every image must abide by this rule. And this helps us understand why literature, guardian of every space haunted by phantoms, has so adroitly searched out those fugitive idols and restored them to their pedestals.

And the mirror? Mightn't that too be inhabited? Let's take a look. Along the frame we see the perennial pursuit, tussle, and flight of gods, Nymphs, and fabled beasts. In the center—on the surface of the mirror—a vast, deep emptiness, where seven bright points tremble, like seven pupils: they are the reflection of the Ursa Major, the Great Bear, and thus of the seven Saptarṣis who keep watch over the cosmos and are its ever wakeful consciousness. Once again Mallarmé has gone back to something before the gods, for the Saptarṣis are also the seven breaths that, uniting together, compose Prajāpati. All that is going on in the soft gilt glow of the mirror's frame—the divine melee—as likewise all that is going on in the darkness of the night outside the windows—the world, which is itself a frame—is equally open to their gaze. Which is the pure fact of consciousness, cut off from all else. Did Mallarmé mean to allude to the Saptarṣis? Wasn't it only years later that he began to read some Indian texts? It's unlikely that we will ever know for certain. But does it matter? The Saptarṣis belong to the Ursa Major: one only need rediscover them. Where the constellation is, there they are. And what can we say of the mirror they appear in? Here it's hard not to see a reference to the Venetian mirror Mallarmé himself was engulfed in, as he described, during his first exploration of the shadow lands of literature. One day, he told his friend Cazalis, he saw himself again in that mirror "the same person I had forgotten months before." But this having been absent from the mirror would be one of the premises underlying all his poetry. The sonnet records the continuing absence of the poet. And as we read it, words that had seemed obscure now ring out to us with sudden clarity: "a disposition of the Spiritual Universe to see itself and develop itself, through what I was." Isn't it this that has found its "objective correlative" in the sonnet? What is left is the world (the night sensed without), an empty room (the hollow shell, as it were, of the vanished author), and the reflection of the seven stars in a mirror, *"de scintillations le septuor"*: thus the mind manifests itself, nor will its wakefulness ever be more sharply discernible.

VI

Mallarmé in Oxford

On March 1st, 1894, in Oxford, and before an audience of about sixty people, dotted here and there with a few professors but mainly made up, as he himself would put it, of ladies "looking for a chance to hear spoken French," Mallarmé gave the lecture generally known as "La Musique et les Lettres." Having been invited to give "some information on various aspects of the current state of literature," he took this journalistic task quite literally and began with an announcement that sounded like a newspaper headline:

"In fact I bring news. The most surprising news. Nothing like this has ever happened. *On a touché au vers*. Verse is under attack."

There is a wonderful irony in that *on*, for as with the report of some terrorist attack, an uncertainty over the perpetrator increases our sense of terror. And then that *touché*—such a physical verb! And one that presupposes, for verse, a previous state of untouchability. Whereas now apparently it is entering a phase of promiscuity. Mallarmé then proceeds with his parody of a front page, but this time taking the leader column as his model: "Governments change; prosody remains ever intact: whether because during revolutions it passes unobserved, or because the attack doesn't imply that this ultimate dogma may change." Then he apologized for his jerky and breathless delivery, like someone who has seen an accident and is desperate to talk about it, with a distress proportional to the gravity of the event: "for verse is everything, to those who write." Mallarmé doesn't say "to those who are poets"; he says "to those who write." Premise: prose itself is "a broken verse, which plays with its timbres and its concealed rhymes too." The statement is followed by a few technicalities, then a final flicker: "for every soul is a rhythmical knot."

Let's take a closer look at the sequence of gestures in this piece of pure mental theatre, something that after all is Mallarmé's chosen discipline. Invited to speak on the subject of "French poetry" as if at an evening school, and preceded—for those few in the know—by a reputation for being one of the least accessible of poets, Mallarmé begins with an announcement that might be written in block capitals on the front page of an evening paper. A few lines later he declares, or implies, one of his most radical ideas: that prose doesn't exist, that everything is verse, whether easily recognizable as such or not; then he winds up with one of those radiant formulations to which he alone knew the secret: the soul is a "rhyth-mical knot." Those who cannot, in the succession of these three scenes, grasp Mallarmé's "flower"—and I use the word in the sense it had for Zeami, founder of Noh theatre—are not likely to grasp it in one of his sonnets.

But let's try to reconstruct the events Mallarmé was eager to bring news of. Behind it all is the death, in 1885, of Victor Hugo. It marked an abrupt turning point in the secret history of literature. Mallarmé spoke of it thus in *Crise de vers*:

> In performing his mysterious task, Hugo channeled all prose, philosophy, eloquence, and history into verse, and since he personally was that verse, he more or less confiscated the right of those who think, discuss, or narrate to make themselves heard. Monument in this desert, with silence far away; in a crypt the divinity of a majestic, uncon-scious idea: that the form called verse is simply itself literature; that verse occurs as soon as diction is marked, rhythm as soon as we have style. Verse, I believe, waited respectfully for the giant who had caused it to be identified with his iron hand and ever firmer blacksmith's grip to die before breaking up. All language articulated with metrics, whence it draws its vital rhythms, escapes in a free disjunc-tion of thousands of simple elements.

If literary history were capable of saying what it is that happens in literature, this is how it would speak. In a few lines Mallarmé has told the story of that movement, first centripetal, then centrifugal, which governs the French language, before him, and then after him down to the present day. Centripetal: Hugo appropriates all the forms in his smoky forge. In so doing he leads us to understand that verse incorporates all of literature in itself. Centrifugal: when Hugo dies, literature seizes the opportunity to escape from the magic circle of meter, no longer guarded by the powerful Cyclops, and to disperse "in a free disjunction of thousands of simple elements." First symptom of this new phase: some young poets begin to champion, often with naïve arrogance, the practice of *vers libre*. Mallarmé knows better than anyone else that *vers libre* is no great discovery. On the contrary, he knows that to speak of liberty in literature is out of place—and so suggests (ingeniously) that this new verse be called "polymorphous" instead. But he doesn't discourage the young poets; for he sees in them the first agents of a healthy shake-up following the "fragmentation of the great literary rhythms." All at once the poetic meters, and even their "definitive jewel," the alexandrine, are no more than noble flotsam and jetsam bobbing about in the mix like some "old and worn-out cast," while already Laforgue is inviting his readers to submit to "the sure enchantment of false verse." Now a "deft dissonance" becomes an attraction for the delicate sensibility, where once it would have been condemned out of hand in a rage of pedantry. And something similar was going on in music too: an exacerbated chromaticism was tormenting tonality, emptying it from within, until eventually the Viennese would reject it altogether.

But these developments were also to be seen in the light of another piece of traumatic news that once again Mallarmé felt it important to report. This time, and with the most studied carelessness, the occasion he chose for his announcement was a survey carried out on behalf of the *Echo de Paris* by the providential journalist Jules Huret, to whom Mallarmé spoke thus:

> Verse occurs whenever there is rhythm in language, which is to say everywhere but on posters and the advertising page of the newspapers. There are verses in the genre called prose, sometimes wonderful verses and in every rhythm. But to tell the truth, prose doesn't exist: there is the alphabet and then there is verse, which may be more or less tight, more or less diffuse. Every time there is a strain toward style, there is versification.

Thus does Mallarmé turn all the terms in the argument on their heads with a boldness incomparably greater than that of the proponents of free verse. In just a couple of sentences verse is made to take on a physiognomy that would hitherto have been unthinkable: we no longer have canonical verse with its established metrics, nor even the amorphous free verse, but an all-pervasive, ubiquitous being which turns out to be the hidden nerve structure of every composition made of words. If the integrity of a respectful and canonical versification is forever wounded by this attack, and if it now seems that prose "doesn't exist" at all, then what is left? Literature, but in what is now its new avatar: sparkling everywhere, like an all-enfolding spiral of dust, and subject to a "dispersal in articulate shivers akin to instrumentation."

Such a radical development could hardly be attributed to a few callow young poets trying out new voices. They were just one sign of a vast and silent upheaval, the first hint of the fact that an immediate correspondence between style and society was no longer possible now. Mallarmé tried to explain as much to his interviewer in the plainest, most straightforward terms: "Above all what has gone is the unquestionable notion that in a society with neither stability nor unity one cannot create a stable art, a definitive art." Hence "the restlessness of minds"; hence "the unexplained need for individuality of which contemporary literary manifestations are the direct reflection." A formidable sociologist when he chose to be, Mallarmé was far more interested in another order of events that was taking shape: the now evident incapacity of the community to create a style for itself would give style the chance—perhaps this is what it had always been waiting for—to free itself, to escape *outside* the society which hitherto had always exploited it for its own ends. Now in contrast a new and unknown land was opening up: the land of the "rhythmical knots," a place where forms are freed from obedience to any authority and rest entirely on themselves.

The claims Mallarmé makes for prose, in his interview with Huret, are presented without demonstration, yet they carry immediate conviction. But can we demonstrate their truth? Let me try to approach the question with an example. In the *Spleen de Paris* Baudelaire has three prose pieces with the same title and subject matter as three of the poems in the *Fleurs du mal*. One of these is the famous "Invitation au voyage." The poem is perfect, fused together like a Vermeer, every syllable pervaded by that "dose of natural opium, incessantly secreted and renewed," that "every man has in him"—but with which Baudelaire had been more generously endowed than most. The *poème en prose*, written some time later, follows the poem step by step, but is much less effective and sometimes ponderous, at least for those who know the poem. But it's hard to see why. Putting the two texts side by side, we find that many of the same images and *tournures* appear in both. Yet the prose piece has a flaw: it is at once lyrical and lavishly detailed. The lines of the poem, on the other hand, are sober and laconic. There are various points where it really would not be possible to offer a *simpler* version. Take, for example, the description of the furniture that would grace the place of happiness the piece evokes. The poem says: "Des meubles luisants, / Polis par les ans, / Décoreraient notre chambre." The prose piece says: "Huge, odd, bizarre furniture bristling like subtle souls with locks and secrets. The mirrors, the metal fittings, the upholstery, the precious items and the majolica-ware play a mute and mysterious symphony for the eyes; and every single thing from every single corner, from the chinks in the drawers and the creases in the upholstery, gives off a special perfume, a Sumatran essence, that is as it were the soul of the apartment." Here the accumulation of detail dilutes the effect. It's hard to decide what to criticize most: whether the likening of the furniture to "subtle souls," merely on account of the locks; or perhaps even worse, the idea of the various objects playing "a mute and mysterious symphony for the eyes"; or the punctiliousness with which we are told that a certain exotic perfume would be "the soul of the apartment," where the word "apartment" with its cruel reminder of land registers and property laws deals the coup de grâce to any enchantment the piece might have had. The prose version is further flawed by a number of tactless remarks that aren't there in the verse. In the first line of the poem the woman invited on the journey is evoked with a definitive "Mon enfant, ma soeur," to which nothing need be added. In the prose, on the other hand, she is first referred to as "une vieille amie," something that already sounds like a gaffe, while later on and with steadily increasing blandness she will become "mon cher ange," then "la femme aimée," and at last "la soeur d'élection" (where that *élection* is another detail we didn't need). The use of the adjective *profond* is likewise a telltale sign: in the prose it turns up twice—which is already once too often, especially given the mention of the "profondeurs du ciel"—and what's more, only three lines apart, first to refer to the sound of the clocks, then to some paintings that are to decorate the rooms of those absent: "Blessed, calm, and profound as the souls of the artists who created them." The poem on the other hand speaks only of there being "miroirs profonds" in these rooms. And at once we are struck by how much more intense and mysterious those two words are than the cumbersome piling-up of adjectives the prose offers, aggravated, what's more, by another appearance of the word *âme*, this time in the plural.

One could go on with the comparison, but already the evidence is damning. Still, we mustn't fall into the trap of thinking this is merely a question of prolixity versus concision, poeticizing—enemy of all literature—versus sobriety. Even less should we conclude that verse is intrinsically superior to prose: indeed it would be all too easy to find a reverse example of a redundant poem that ruins the sober dispatch of a note made in prose. The reason I offered this example has to do with Mallarmé's theory as to the nonexistence of prose. If the lines of the "Invitation" are incomparably more attractive than the version in prose, it is first and foremost because the sovereign power of meter is so strongly at work in them, because the lines are held tight in the gentle pincers of meter and rhyme: two five-syllable lines with a masculine rhyme, followed by a seven-syllable line with feminine rhyme, where the sharpness of the masculine rhymes—like points of a triangle—are answered by the slight dip of the feminine rhymes. And this berceuse, rocking as gently as a boat of *humeur vagabonde* that you might see in some canal in Amsterdam, European storehouse of Oriental spice—this movement that is barely hinted at, yet perceptible with Flemish clarity, makes every single word its prisoner, so that they can't expand even by a single syllable, they can't launch into the explanation that kills, with what Verlaine called "la Pointe assassine."

But what happens in the prose version? Does it really have, as Mallarmé's argument suggests, a hidden and unnamed meter? And if it does, wouldn't that contradict Baudelaire's own claims, for in the dedication to Houssaye that opens the *Spleen de Paris* he presents the work as an example of "a poetic prose, musical without rhythm and without rhyme"? "Without rhythm": that sounds like a thesis that is the direct opposite of Mallarmé's—as if prose were seeking to conquer the territory of poetry without bowing to the yoke of meter. But it's well known that declarations of poetics all too often turn out to be traps lovingly set by writers for their readers. So it was that Gianfranco Contini's analytical lancet would one day identify, in the very first paragraph of that remarkable declaration of intent, a weave of alexandrine hemistiches culminating, in the last sentence, in a pure alexandrine: "J'ose vous dédier le serpent tout entier." And that's not all. Extending his inquiry to the *poèmes en prose* themselves, Contini found numerous other alexandrine hemistiches, and most outstanding of all "a complete alexandrine, indeed one of the most extraordinary Baudelaire ever wrote: 'au loin je ne sais quoi avec ses yeux de marbre.'" Or a slightly irregular alexandrine like: "Que les fins de journées d'automne sont pénétrantes." And he eventually reaches the conclusion that the whole of the *Spleen de Paris* was "drenched in internal alexandrines." But what happens when, as with "Invitation au voyage," the prose is based on a model in verse that "has no relationship with the alexandrine"? We have already seen the semantic consequences, a tendency to amplify that dissolves the magic formula of the verse in a slow wave, whose charm is less intense, albeit still there. Now, Contini's fine ear succeeded in pinning down the *numerus* of that wave: "So much sumptuousness allows of but one interpretation, which might concisely be described thus: the transformation of the 'Invitation' into an equivalent of the poem in alexandrines." As if Baudelaire had once again obeyed an obscure compulsion that drove him to *say everything* in alexandrines. Only in this meter would the *lingua adamica* articulate itself. So in the two versions of the "Invitation" the struggle is not between meter and prose "without rhythm," as Baudelaire would have it, but between two different meters. And, for once, the alexandrine is beaten by the berceuse—something all the more remarkable when one considers that, as Contini put it, "Baudelaire speaks naturally in alexandrines or fragments of alexandrines, even where he tones them down and breaks them up." The alexandrines within the *Spleen de Paris* thus confirm, in a sort of proof *ab absurdo*, the thesis put forward by Mallarmé.

But did Mallarmé merely want to tell us that meter was everywhere present in prose? Or was he trying to get at something at once more subtle and more serious? Let's go back to the most surprising moments of the interview as reported by Huret: "To tell the truth, prose doesn't exist: there is the alphabet and then there is verse, which may be more or less tight, more or less diffuse." It's hard at first to grasp the full—indeed, as we shall gradually appreciate, immense—consequences of these remarks. Like opium, as Baudelaire describes it, they have the power to "stretch out the unlimited." The landscape that now opens up before us has two extremes: on the one hand, the alphabet; on the other, rhythm. And rhythm means meter. One's immediate thought is that language, which until a moment ago was strutting center stage, has disappeared. Then we find it again, as a pure material that appears and continually migrates back and forth from one extreme to another. The relationships have changed: meter is no longer a mere function of language, but rather the contrary: language comes into being as a function of meter. It is only thanks to meter that we have style. And only thanks to style that we have literature. Consequently: any distinction between prose and poetry is insubstantial. They are just different degrees within the same continuum. Whether easy to recognize or not, rhythm is always the underlying power that governs the word, as if the literary depended most of all on a tension between this nonverbal, gestural, urgent element and the articulation of the word itself. What's more, if "prose doesn't exist," one might equally well say that poetry doesn't exist either. So what is left? Literature.

Mallarmé had put this as clearly as it can be put: "The form called verse is simply itself literature." But he also said that until Hugo's death this truth had been hidden away like a divinity in a crypt, where "like a majestic, unconscious idea" it caused literature to weave a sort of secret dream around itself. Now that dream had burst out into the light. This was what Mallarmé was thinking of when he wrote that the end of the century had seen a "fretting of the veil in the temple, with significant folds and even some tearing." The words were still ringing in Yeats's ears when he entitled the first part of his *Autobiographies* "The Trembling of the Veil." And ringing still louder the evening of the première of *Ubu Roi,* when he said to some friends: "After Stéphane Mallarmé, after Paul Verlaine, after Gustave Moreau, after Puvis de Chavannes, after our own verse, after all our subtle colour and nervous rhythm, after the faint mixed tints of Conder, what more is possible? After us the Savage God."

Though it is with a certain incredulity, a century on, that one tries to imagine Puvis de Chavannes ever having had such a subversive power, all the same we can't help hearing in Yeats's words the striking, overheated chord of a new era. And especially when we see Mallarmé cited as the leading name in the list.

At this point it becomes increasingly clear how Mallarmé had seen and grasped, behind the claims of *vers*

libre, a far more momentous event, one that manifested itself "for the first time in the literary history of
any people": the possibility, that is, for each individual, "with his own way of playing and his own individual ear, to fashion an instrument for himself, as
soon as he blows, touches, or beats it with science." In
other words, *an escape from the rhetorical canon*,
which was not to be rejected as such, only that it no
longer had any power to bind and could no longer
claim to be the voice of the community. At best the
whole of rhetoric could now expect the same fate that
awaited the alexandrine: as the "national cadence" it
could be waved like a flag, at festivals and special cel-
ebrations. But to abandon the fortress of rhetoric did
not, for Mallarmé, mean one need plunge into an
amorphous maelstrom. On the contrary, what flashed
before his vision was a literature where the power of
form would be raised to an even higher level. True,
form would be cut loose now from everything else, it
would be more arduously encoded than it had been in
the past; but perhaps precisely because of that it
might also get closer to the underlying ground of our
experience, since "There must be something occult in
the ground of everyone." This unprecedented literature opened out before him like a vast surface for possible combinations to form upon, a surface composed
of letters and strewn with meters—whole, broken,
obvious, disguised. So just when meter itself was

being discredited as the voice of the community, the single meters, the single physiological feet of rhythm, became the hidden *numerus* and animating force of all literature, which was now entering a phase that would be "polymorphic" in the extreme. And yet nothing could have been more alien to Mallarmé than the cavalier gesturing of the avant-garde. Certainly the situation had forced upon everyone a "newly acquired liberty." Yet something else needed saying too, and Mallarmé says it in a tone as calm as it is severe: "I cannot see, and this remains my firm opinion, that anything that was beautiful in the past is canceled out by this." What did change radically was the strategic position of the word "literature." On the one hand, it was rendered superfluous and ineffective by the flood of "universal *reportage*" that suffocated it; but at the same time, it was catapulted into a "new heaven and a new earth." And this was at once the most disturbing news and the most difficult to grasp. Mallarmé places it at the center of his Oxford lecture. And he approaches it with maximum caution, solicitously advising his audience that it is surely an "exaggeration":

"Yes, Literature exists and, if you like, alone, an exception from everything."

More than any debate about free verse, this statement really was shocking. In his characteristic manner, "a bit like a priest, a bit like a ballerina," and with his infinitely delicate and intimidating diction,

Mallarmé gave notice that having left by society's front door, literature was coming back in through a cosmic window, having absorbed in the meantime nothing less than everything. Those words marked the end of a long, meandering story. And they celebrated the moment when a daring fiction took shape and crystallized, a fiction from which the whole of the century to come would draw sustenance, and from which we still draw sustenance today: absolute literature.

VII

"Meters Are the Cattle of the Gods"

Meters are the cattle of the gods," we read in the *Śatapatha Brāhmaṇa*. This was *the* premise, something we find hard to understand today. When we think of meters, we may perhaps glimpse the vague outline of a rhythm, but not much more. Yet it wasn't always thus, and certainly not for the Vedic seers, the *ṛṣis* who composed the Rgveda. To understand what meters are, they thought, one must go back to the gods and beyond the gods, as far as Prajāpati, the Progenitor, that indefinite being who has no name of his own, unless we count as a name the interrogative pronoun Ka (Who?), that unlimited being out of whom the gods themselves sprang. Yet even the Father had been born together with "evil," *pāpman*, that evil which is "death," *mṛtyu*: "While Prajāpati was creating, Death, that evil, overcame him." Thus the gods were born mortal; the fear of death dwelt within them. "Prajāpati constructed the fire; it was keen-edged as a razor; terrified, the gods would not come near; then, wrapping themselves in the meters, they came near, and that is how the meters got their name. The meters are sacred power; the skin of the black antelope is the form of sacred power; he puts on shoes of antelope skin; not to be hurt, he wraps himself in meters before approaching the fire." The "meters," *chandas,* are the robes that the gods "wrapped around themselves," *acchādayan,* so that they might come near to the fire without being disfigured as though by the blade of a razor. Thus the gods sought to escape death. And likewise men—for men always tell themselves: "I must do as the gods did." When the *Taittirīya Saṃhitā* says, "He wraps himself in meters before coming near the fire, so as not to be hurt," it is referring to any priest, any man. Today, seen through eyes no longer familiar with rites and with fire, the phrase cannot help but make us think of what, consciously or otherwise, every poet, every writer does when he writes. And of at least one poet I know that this was quite literally true: Joseph Brodsky. When Brodsky spoke of meter, and of the imminent danger that we might forget what meter is, his voice would be tense, as though he were speaking of a mortal peril, speaking precisely, for sure, and soberly, but also with the pathos that a perilous situation demands.

But why are the meters so tremendously important, so much so that even the gods needed them to protect themselves? Everything that exists is permeated by two invisible powers—"mind," *manas,* and "word," *vāc,* a twinned pair whose distinguishing characteristic is that they are at once "equal," *samāna*, and "distinct," *nānā*. The work of ritual—and thus any *work*—consists above all in making sure that this characteristic is not lost in pure indistinction. Thus "mind" and "word" are assigned slightly different ritual utensils: for the one a ladle must be used; for the other a wooden spoon with a curved beak. And two different libations are offered, that "are mind and word: thus he [the officiant] separates mind and word one from the other; and thus mind and word, though equal, *samāna*, are nevertheless distinct, *nānā*." In one respect, however, mind and word are drastically different: in their extension. "Mind is far more unlimited and word is far more limited." These two entities belong to two different levels of being, but to operate effectively they must team up, *yoke themselves together*. Mind alone, word alone, are impotent—or at least not powerful enough to take an offering to the gods. The horse of the mind must submit to the harness of the word, of the meters: otherwise it would lose its way.

But how can two such disproportionate beings be yoked together? "When one of the pair in the yoke is smaller, they give it an extra support bar . . . so he gives a support bar to the word, and like well-paired companions yoked together these two now take the sacrifice to the gods." That support bar is a subtle metaphysical contrivance—and it is only thanks to that contrivance that the offering has ever been able to reach the gods. Reminding ourselves of its origin will help us understand why the word is never whole, but always flawed in some way or composite, threatened by its own lack of substance—or in any case its insufficient weight.

But what about meter? Meter is the *yoke* of the word. Just as the "mind," *manas*, is so flighty in its movements—a monkey leaping from branch to branch—that it would be quite dispersed if it did not accept a yoke (and every mental discipline, every *yoga*, is above all a "yoke"); so the "word," *vāc*, omnipresent, pervasive, which "blows like the wind, sweeping across all worlds," bows to the restrictions of meter, agrees to dress up in it as if in colorful clothes, to be wrapped up, as it were, in a preordained arrangement of syllables. Only thus can it reach the heavens, like a female creature covered in bird feathers. And only thus can it make the return journey from heaven to earth. Such facility, such familiarity with different worlds, inevitably makes us wonder: could it be that rather than just leading us to the gods, the meters *are* the gods themselves? After that thought has occurred, we won't be surprised when we come across these words: "Now, the gods who govern life are the meters, for it is thanks to the meters that all living things here below are sustained." With respect to the thirty-three Devas, the meters play a double role, at once subordinate and sovereign: humble and useful like beasts of burden who "when yoked carry weights for men, so the meters, when yoked, carry the sacrifice to the gods." But at the same time only the meters can get close to the fire without being harmed. And above all: if the gods have achieved immortality, it is the meters they have to thank for it. Once the gods roamed the earth—yearning for the sky. They knew that it was there immortality was to be found. But they didn't know how to get there. Then Gāyatrī, the female creature who is the shortest and most effective of the meters, transformed herself into a *śyena*, a hawk or eagle. In that form she managed to steal from the sky the substance death cannot harm: *soma*. But hers wasn't the first attempt. Two other meters had tried and failed before her: Jagatī, who lost three syllables in the process; then Triṣṭubh, who lost one. When Gāyatrī reappeared, with the *soma* in her beak, her body was made up of her own four syllables plus those her sisters had lost. Meantime the arrow of a mysterious archer, a celestial guardian, had ruffled her plumage and torn off a leaf of the *soma* plant. Loss and wound thus lurked within the meter that must heal loss and wound. From then on Gāyatrī, Triṣṭubh, and Jagatī would always follow King Soma. A king can hardly turn up unattended. So who forms his retinue? The meters. "Just as dignitaries, heralds, and captains stand beside the king, so the meters move about him like servants." Like K.'s assistants in Kafka's *The Castle*, the meters go wherever Soma goes. Soma arrives on a chariot carrying the branches of a plant that "grows in the mountains." But alongside the chariot, those who know will also see the gleam of the meters, like rays around the sun.

But there is a danger inherent in the life of the meters. Ceremonies sap their strength. Always last in everything, by the time men found the meters they had already been used up by the gods; they were worn out: "Now the strength of the meters was exhausted by the gods, because it was through the meters that the gods reached the heavens. And the chant is rapture, *mada*: the rapture that is in *ṛc* and in *sāman*, which is sap, and that sap he now injects into the meters and so restores their strength; and with their vigor now renewed the sacrifice is celebrated." If we wanted to know why inspiration is necessary, here at last is an explanation. That "rapture" which we call *inspiration* is the only resource we have for reviving the meters, worn out as they are by the rash use they were once put to, not by men but by the gods. Without that "rapture" the meters would remain inert, like plants longing to be watered, mute testimony to that exploit which, through the power of a body of syllables, made the gods immortal.

If the gods reached the heavens through a form, how much more will men have need of form if they are to reach the gods. And only the meters will allow men to become creatures who, though mortal, know how to use the forms the gods used. The meters are our *témenos*, the form within which all forms appear. As if coming to us through a bright mist (the one Bloomfield called the "Vedic haze," perhaps?), all this strikes a chord, even for the reader in the West who knows nothing of Vedic rituals. It is as if those rituals had immediately developed and indeed pushed to its ultimate consequences something that in the West was to nourish not so much ritual as that extraterritorial and elusive creature we call literature. Now we begin to see why literature is so often connected to immortality, and in a sense far more radical than the, to tell the truth, rather modest achievement of being remembered by future generations.

And only now do we see why for all its many metamorphoses there is one element that literature seems never to relinquish: form. Yet it is never too explicit in laying claim to it either, nor does it seek to establish its sovereignty. Which makes us wonder: what is the myth of form? And for some time we search for it in vain, albeit convinced that, as for every other essential entity, form must have its myth. Greece offers us only the Muses, who are not so much figures of form as delicate hints of the power that every form emanates: possession, that knowledge shared by Dionysus and Apollo at Delphi, whose premise is that the mind is a hollow space constantly invaded by gods and voices. The Muses, who are above all Nymphs *rangées*—well-behaved Nymphs, that is—make sure that the forms do in fact take possession of us and cause us to speak following rules that may be more or less occult, the way music, Leibniz thought, is governed by an occult mathematics. But if the Muses are the supreme well-springs and custodians of forms, who are the forms themselves? Another group of female creatures: the meters who turned themselves into birds with bodies made of syllables.

It was the Vedic seers who chanted them and exercised them without cease. And it is to those seers that the cult of form, in its purest, most abstract, and most penetrating version goes back. Nor did they stop at that, but went so far as to foreshadow every claim to the self-sufficiency—even autism—of the poetic word. For since the elaboration and refinement of the word, its becoming *saṃskṛta*, "perfected," and thus Sanskrit, was likened in the hymns of the Ṛgveda to every sort of activity—from the harnessing of horse and cart, to weaving, anointment, grooming, milking, cooking, seafaring—and since the Vedic seers "assimilate and confound what they compare, not having the impression that the image is a notion objectively heterogeneous to the thing that prompted it," the practice of the hymns leads to a condition where everything that is said of the object is also applied to the word that names it; or at least one observes a "constant slippage from one register to the other." So much so that "one could argue that the whole Ṛgveda is an allegory." But an allegory of what? Of itself. So Mallarmé's sonnet "in *ix*," which the author himself said was "allegorical of itself," turns out to be a sharpened splinter of light gleaming back into the past so far as to shine on that collection of hymns thought to be primordial and "nonhuman," *apauruṣeya*: the Ṛgveda.

In order to make such extreme and all-embracing claims for the word of the hymns, the Vedic seers had to have a solid "base," *pratiṣṭhā*. No, more than solid: unshakable. And that base was the syllable. First and foremost they were makers not of words but of syllables. Syllables were the *prima materia* of their alchemy. If Mallarmé would remark on the wondrous phenomenon by which any fact transforms itself into its "almost vanishing vibration," Vedic doctrine had long before superimposed on that a second and no less wondrous phenomenon: the evanescent sound substance of the syllable was celebrated as the indestructible, "the nonfluent," *akṣara*. One can squeeze a juice, a "flavor," *rasa*, from anything, says the *Jaiminīya Upaniṣad Brāhmaṇa*. But not from the syllable: because the syllable is itself the juice of everything. It thus lives on—untarnished, inexhaustible. And from the syllable all else flows. Or rather, only the syllable allows everything to be fluid, vivid. Motionless before the barrier that was the rock of Vala, the Aṅgiras uttered syllables. And those syllables they chanted split the rock. From the fissure burst forth the hidden Cows, the Waters. Nor have they ever stopped flowing. For if they did the world would stiffen in paralysis. This is the premise behind the Vedic meter, which is syllabic, not quantitative. Everything forms from combinations of different numbers of these sound molecules. And a mysterious allusion tells us that "what for men is a number, for the gods is a syllable." But what is a "syllable," *akṣara*? While in modern languages "syllable" has no connotations beyond the phonetic, the Sanskrit *akṣara* belongs to that narrow circle of words, like *brahman*, where an ungovernable drift of meanings overwhelms a hypothetical first meaning—hypothetical because eventually we begin to wonder if there is such a meaning, or in any event whether it can claim priority. The most obvious example is *brahman*, where the first meaning might be "ritual formula" or "enigma," as Louis Renou and Lilian Silburn have maintained. But the Saint Petersburg Dictionary listed seven meanings. In the case of the *akṣara*, the priority of the meaning "syllable" is clear enough, as the whole of hymn 164 of the first *maṇḍala*—or "circle"—of the Ṛgveda suggests. And on this the first commentaries we have agree.

Etymologists of ancient times understood *akṣara* to be that which *na kṣarati*, "does not flow," with a privative prefix *a*. And for once modern linguists agree. Including Mayrhofer, who only adds a parallel with the Greek *phtheírō*, "to corrupt" and "to destroy," whence *áphthartos, unvergänglich*, and so the Italian *imperituro*, or the English "imperishable," which, from a certain moment on, was to be the dominant if not exclusive meaning of *akṣara*.

The syllable is that which remains unscathed. When the woman theologian Gārgī challenged Yājñavalkya in the highest and most tense duel of thought of which we have record—and not even the Greece of the sages and sophists produced its like—the stern, brusque seer was asked to name the weft on which different things were woven, for Gārgī was a famous weaver. Eleven times Yājñavalkya answered her, naming the weft of the water, the winds, the atmosphere, the worlds of the Gandharvas, the worlds of the sun, the worlds of the moon, the worlds of the constellations, the worlds of the gods, the worlds of Indra, the worlds of Prajāpati, the worlds of *brahman*. At which point he in turn challenged Gārgī: "Do not ask too much, take care that your head doesn't burst." But Gārgī was fearless, and pressed on. She said: "That which, oh Yājñavalkya, is above the sky, that which is beneath the earth, that which is between the sky and the earth, that which is called past, present, and future, upon what weft is this woven?" Yājñavalkya replied: "On the ether, *ākāśa*." But this still wasn't enough: "'And the ether, what is that woven on?' He answered: 'In truth, oh Gārgī, on this *akṣara* [on the syllable, on the imperishable], of which the brahmans say that it is neither thick nor thin, neither short nor long, neither flame nor liquid, neither colored nor dark, neither wind nor ether, it doesn't stick, is without taste, without smell, without eyes, without ears, without voice, without mind, without heat, without breath, without mouth, without measure, without an inside, without an outside. It does not eat and is not eaten.'"

Yājñavalkya's words mark the turning point in the history of the *akṣara*: from now on this neuter noun that means "syllable" would appear in the texts as an adjective meaning "imperishable," and thus effacing the "syllable." But originally the two meanings coincided. How do we know? The Ṛgveda tells us: "When the ancient Dawns rose, the Great Syllable [*mahed akṣaram*] was born in the footprint of the Cow." "Footprint" is a translation of *pada*, a key word in the enigmatic lexicon of which the Ṛgveda is woven, and it means "foot," "paw," or even "limb, articulation" of a line of verse, and finally "step" or "footprint." As for the cow, and again drawing on the enigmatic lexicon, this is Vāc, Word, *Vox*. And "Vāc is *gāyatrī*, because

Vāc sings [*gāyati*] and protects [*trāyate*] all this [universe]." Even as it issues forth, then, the syllable is already meter, as another hymn by enigmas will hint: "The wild Cow lowed as it fashioned the flowing waters; it became of one *pada*, of two *padas*, of eight *padas*, of nine *padas*, of a thousand syllables in the supreme place. From her flow the seas, on her live the four regions of the world. On the syllable that flows from her [*kṣaraty akṣaram*] lives all this [universe]."

"The nonflowing that flows," *kṣaraty akṣaram*: it is on these two words that the enigma converges, as if all the fluidity of life were made possible only by something that doesn't flow. The syllable is the meeting point between pure vibration and form, the meter.

The syllable, the meter, the word: the circle expands. But it doesn't close. For that to happen the syllable must be answered by its counterpart: the fire. The syllable is effective only if spoken before and in counterpoint to the fire. At every kindling of the fire, as the sacrificer rubs the two pieces of wood together, a chant can be heard in the background, the *sāman* that gives new vigor, while "the hotar holds himself ready to start reciting the appropriate mantras at the first wisp of smoke that will rise from the lower drilling block. When the drilling fails and the smoke disappears, the mantra, too, ceases; to start again when the smoke appears again. One can say that the mantra bears the fire, or that the fire begets the mantra." Only reciprocal generation—as between Puruṣa and Virāj, at once goddess and meter—can serve as an account of the relationship between the meters and the fire. Gāyatrī is a robe that wraps and protects from the sharp blades of the flame. But Gāyatrī is also a "firebrand," *samidh*: "Gāyatrī, when kindled, kindles the other meters; and once kindled the meters bring the sacrifice to the gods." It is said of Agni Jātavedas, Fire Knower-of-Creatures, that he sparks within the syllable, in that most arcane of places, which is "the matrix of order," *ṛtásya yónim*.

Only an intimacy, a mingling, a superimposition as extreme as that between the syllable and the fire can guarantee the continuity of the world for the moment. This is the ultimate enigma behind all the ciphered names: the "imperishable" consists of a sound sustained by a transitory breath and in a devouring blaze that will go out as soon as no fuel is fed to it. The imperishable is what most appears to be ephemeral. The continuous is entrusted to a breath that may run out at any moment and to a flame that an unknown hand must constantly tend. But that is precisely what the rites are for: to weave continuity. Otherwise life would fall apart in broken stumps. Above all this is what the meters are for: to give continuous measure to our breathing. Otherwise how would we know when to take a breath? The *Śatapatha Brāhmaṇa* observes: 'If [the officiant] took a breath halfway through a line, there would be a crack in the sacrifice": it would be a first defeat at the hands of the discontinuous, which would force its way into the middle of the line like a wedge. To make sure that doesn't happen, one must at least recite the lines of the *gāyatrī*, the shortest of the meters, one by one, without breaking them to take a breath. Thus a tiny, unassailable cell of continuity will be formed in the serrated extension of the discontinuous.

Passing the baton like relay runners, the meters act first and foremost upon time; *they make sure that it isn't interrupted*: "Above all he recites the verses in a continuous way: thus he makes the days and nights of the years continuous, and thus the days and nights of the year alternate in a continuous, uninterrupted way. And in this way he leaves no path open to the evil enemy; in fact he would leave one path open, therefore, if he recited the lines jerkily; he recites them smoothly without interruptions." What emerges quite dramatically here is the Vedic officiant's overriding anxiety: the fear that time will be broken, that the day's progress will suddenly be interrupted, that the whole world may be left in a state of irretrievable dispersion. This fear is far more radical than the fear of death. Or rather, the fear of death is a secondary manifestation of it—a modern manifestation, we might say. Something else precedes it: a sense of precariousness so extreme, intense, and lacerating as to make the

continuity of time appear as an improbable gift forever on the point of being withdrawn. So it is that one
must act at once by making the sacrifice, which we
can define as that thing which the officiant *tends*,
extends. This weave from an indeterminate material,
this first text, which is the sacrifice, must be "tended,"
tan, so as to form something connected, something
without a tear, or interruption, or break, through
which the "evil enemy" who is always ready to strike
might creep in; something that, because of the elaborate nature of its composition, can stand up against
the world, which presents itself to us as a series of
"isolated" (*pṛthak*) entities, of tears, interruptions,
and fragments, in which we recognize shreds of the
dismembered body of Prajāpati. To overcome the discontinuous: this is the officiant's goal. Conquering
death is just one of the many consequences of that. So
the first requirement is that the *hotṛ*'s voice be, so far
as is possible, tense, a constant issuing of sound. That
is how one day the *gāyatrī* meter became Gāyatrī the
bird and had the power to soar up to the heavens to
conquer Soma, that intoxicating and encompassing
liquid which the officiant recognized as the supreme
expansion of the continuous.

An immense distance separates the *akṣara* from the
lógos of Saint John's Gospel. *Lógos* is articulate dis-
course, a concatenation of meanings. *Akṣara* is the
irreducible vibration that precedes meaning, com-

poses meaning, but is not absorbed into it. When *akṣara*, the Great Syllable, is identified in a sound, that sound is *om*, which is an interjection, not a noun. *Om* is "the syllable that expresses assent." Before stating anything about the world, *akṣara* gestures its acceptance of the world. The very moment it sets out to articulate, the word approves the world. And that moment will remain forever pre-eminent over whatever meaning is then attributed to the world, just as the moment of waking stands out from the flow of consciousness that follows. And still today, "the cry OM! is the commonest sound heard at the sacrifice." An incessant "yes" encompasses every gesture and every word. That "yes" to all existence, which for Nietzsche would coincide with the revelation of the eternal return, had always been there throughout every Vedic rite, its sound halo.

From the syllable one passed, imperceptibly, into the meters. The Vedic meters were the first example of the worship of form. And it was a pure form, an empty form that preceded any meaning because itself invested with the highest meaning of all: "Oh Gāyatrī, you have one foot, two feet, three feet, four feet; you do not have feet [*pad*], because you don't fall [you do not perish, *na padyase*]."

But if the meter does not perish, what about those who use it? Mounting on the meters, the gods conquered the heavens—immortality. And men? Beside the "unborn" gods there are gods who achieved their state "with actions." Could men do it too then? "The immortal has the same origin as the mortal," say the hymns. So the Vedic seers didn't exclude this eventuality. But has it ever happened? At least once—or so we are cryptically told. And to three brothers, the Rbhus. Their names were Vāja, Rbhukṣan, Vibhvan. "Sons of men," like everybody else, but unusual for their eyes, because they had "eyes of sun," *suracakṣasaḥ*, like the gods. Their family name includes the *r-* which designates that which is well articulated: above all *ṛta*, the "order" that is "truth." The heraldic word of the Rbhu brothers was *takṣ-*, "to fashion," the same word used to describe the syllable that "fashions" the meters and the waters. Before anything else they were great craftsmen: carpenters, blacksmiths. For the Aśvins they fashioned a three-wheeled chariot that roamed the heavens without reins. They made it "with the mind, with thought," *mánasas pári dhyáyā*. For Indra they caused two bay horses to appear. But they also contributed to the work par excellence, which is the sacrifice: "For Agni the Rbhus fashioned sacred formulas [*bráhma tatakṣuḥ*]," which men then used in their rites. So those who sacrifice today consider themselves "children of the Rbhus."

In the end, with the strength of their works, they conquered the heavens. Not because they were devoted to form, but because they practiced the devotion that is form: "By means of the arts by which you gave form to the cup, by means of the invention by which you made the cow from hide, by means of the thought with which you composed the two bay horses, by means of all this you three Ṛbhus have achieved divine status."

Stella Kramrisch wrote of them: "The Ṛbhus are the archetype of the artist." Of the kind of life they led on earth we know very little: once they fashioned a cow from cowhide and reunited "the mother with the calf." When their parents were left lying on the ground, like "sacrificial poles decomposing," they poured youth back into them.

In the heavens, Indra and the Aśvin twins welcomed the Ṛbhus as friends. They had a great deal in common. But the other gods were generous too, conceding the Ṛbhus the third libation in the sacrifice. This is all the more remarkable since, having achieved immortality, the gods had always been spiteful and treacherous towards men. Never did they show greater zeal than when wiping out the last traces of their successful sacrifice on earth so that men wouldn't be able to follow suit. But this happy ending *in coelestibus* was not, as it turns out, the end of the Ṛbhu brothers' story. That would have been too straightforward, too clear, too unambiguous. And no artist's story is ever straightforward, clear, and unambiguous.

Paradoxically, although they'd made it to the heavens, the Ṛbhus had not yet accomplished their real work. Getting there had just been a preparation. Now came the big gamble. One day, "having wandered about a great deal," the Ṛbhus arrived "in the house of the sacrificer Savitṛ." A little-known god, Savitṛ is the Impeller, the *Agohya*, "he from whom nothing can be hidden." It was Savitṛ who gave the Ṛbhus the seal of immortality. And it was in his house that the Ṛbhus slept for twelve days, a prodigious suspension of time, during the winter solstice. Thanks to that sacred hibernation the grass would sprout again on the earth far away when winter was over. The brothers were woken by a dog, who was the celestial Dog. But the most important thing that happened at Savitṛ's house was that the Ṛbhus, who were human craftsmen, met Tvaṣṭṛ, the divine Craftsman, jealous custodian of the *soma*. Thus began the most mysterious phase of their lives. What we know of it is fragmentary and comes without a shred of explanation. As follows: the cup from which the gods and Tvaṣṭṛ drank the *soma* was unique. It was the only one. The Ṛbhus looked at it, studied it. Then they "reproduced that cup of the Asura [Tvaṣṭṛ] that was unique four times over." How did they do it? By taking careful measurements: using their art, which was *māyā*, "the measuring magic," as the illuminating translation of Lilian Silburn puts it. Tvaṣṭṛ's eyes gaped when he saw "those four cups, shining like new days." And at once he said: "We shall kill them, these men who have profaned the divine cup of the *soma*." Quite what happened next is not clear. Female shadows appear on the scene. Of Tvaṣṭṛ it is said that he took refuge among the wives of the gods. Of the Ṛbhus we hear that "they led the maiden to safety, under another name." But we don't know who the maiden was. Only one thing do we know for sure: those four shining cups, perfect copies of the unique cup, ruined forever the relationship between the gods and those first artists, those first men to share divine immortality. The Ṛbhus had trespassed too far into the place where fetish and reflection grow together and part. So long as the unique exists, the simulacrum is its prisoner within. But no sooner are the cups multiplied than an unstoppable cataract of simulacra rains down from the sky. The world has lived off them ever since—all this was hardly likely to please the gods; for if the copy cancels out the unique, then in the wake of the copy comes death. What are the first simulacra if not images and apparitions of the dead? Which takes us back to that long-lost time when the gods too trod the earth, as mortals. It wasn't something they wanted to be reminded of.

Whoever calls forth the copy performs the most momentous of gestures, in the heavens. Which then resonates on earth. Why did they do it? We are not told. When their friend Agni asked them, the Ṛbhus answered: "We did not profane the cup, which is of noble origin. We only spoke of the way the wood is shaped, brother Agni." They seem to be saying: we were mostly interested in the technical aspects. It is the reply by which one recognizes the artist.

But the gods didn't forgive them. Even their friends, even Agni together with the Vasus, even Indra with the Rudras, even the Viśvedevas, excluded them from the three pressings of the *soma*, at morning, noon, and dusk: "Here you shall not drink, not here." Aloof as ever, Prajāpati looked on. He turned to Savitṛ: "You taught them, you drink with them!" Savitṛ did so, and he in turn invited Prajāpati to drink with the Ṛbhus. Alone with those left alone. As for the gods, they said "the Ṛbhus made them nauseous because of their human smell." One never becomes immortal enough.

VIII

✢✢✢

Absolute Literature

What are writers talking about when they name the gods? If those names are not part of a cult—not even the metaphorical cult that is rhetoric—what is their mode of being? "The gods have become diseases," wrote Jung with illuminating brutality. Like so many refugees from time, they have all taken shelter together in the amorphous psychic mass. But does this diminish them? Mightn't it rather be considered a return to the original state of things—or at least a withdrawal to that enclosed space, to that *témenos*, whence the gods have always sprung? For whatever they may be, the gods manifest themselves above all as mental events. Yet, contrary to the modern illusion, it is the psychic powers that are fragments of the gods, not the gods that are fragments of the psychic powers. If they are thought of as no more than that, the impact can be violent, something we don't know how to speak about except by resorting to the degrading lexicon of pathology. And that's precisely the moment when literature can become an effective stratagem for sneaking the gods out of the universal clinic and getting them back into the world, scattered across its surface where they have always dwelt, since, as the Neoplatonist Salustius wrote, "the world itself can be considered a myth." In these circumstances they may even travel incognito, indistinguishable from anyone else entering or leaving a cosmic Hôtel du Libre Échange; or they may show themselves in their ancient robes in hyper-real decal images. But one way or another the world will go on being the place of epiphanies. And, to travel among them, literature will be the last surviving Pausanias. But are we quite sure we know what "literature" means? When we pronounce the word today, we are immediately aware that it is immeasurably distant from anything an eighteenth-century writer might have meant by it, while at the beginning of the nineteenth century it was already taking on connotations we quickly recognize: notably the most audacious and demanding, those that leave the ancient pattern of genres and prescribed styles far behind, like some kind of kindergarten forever abandoned in a flight towards a knowledge grounded only in itself and expanding everywhere like a cloud, cloaking every shape, overstepping every boundary. This new creature that appeared we don't know quite when and that still lives among us may be defined as "absolute literature." "Literature" because it is a knowledge that claims to be accessible only and exclusively by way of literary composition; "absolute" because it is a knowledge that one assimilates while in search of an absolute, and that thus draws in no less than everything; and at the same time it is something *absolutum*, unbound, freed from any duty or common cause, from any social utility. Sometimes proclaimed with arrogance, elsewhere practiced in secret and with subtle cunning, this knowledge first becomes perceptible in literature, as presence or premonition, in the early days of German Romanticism, and seems destined never to leave it. Like a sort of irreversible mutation, you can celebrate it, you can loathe it, but either way it now belongs to the very physiology of writing.

Resorting to the useful superstition of dates, we could say that the heroic age of absolute literature begins in 1798 with a review, the *Athenaeum*, mostly put together anonymously by a few young men in their early twenties—"proud seraphs," Wieland called them—among whom the names of Friedrich Schlegel and Novalis catch the eye, and ends in 1898 with the death of Mallarmé in Valvins. A century to the year, during which all the decisive traits of absolute literature had occasion to manifest themselves. Which is to say that what came afterwards—embarrassingly labeled as "modernism" or "the avant-garde"—had already lost its auroral brightness, a fact that partly explains why it was so fond of aggressive, disruptive forms, first and foremost of which was the manifesto. By the end of the nineteenth century the essential features of the obscure process were in place. Then came the ramifications, the interlacings, a century of innumerable hybrids, repercussions, invasions of new territories. But how to explain the origins of the process? Certainly not via some historical or sociological approach. For one can't help feeling that the entire phenomenon amounts to the most radical apostasy from history and society. It's as if, exactly as the mesh of society tightened, so as to block out the whole sky, exactly as it clamored ever more loudly for a cult of its own, so the recruitment of a band of recalcitrants began, some of them discreet, some rowdy, some quite unassailable in their rejection—not because they felt duty-bound to other cults, but because possessed by a sense of divinity so intense it had no need to give itself a name, and at the same time so precise as to impose immediate rejection of that poisonous counterfeit that the Great Animal of society (the definition is Plato's) was putting together with such tremendous power and zeal. From Hölderlin to the present day, nothing essential has changed in this regard, except perhaps that society's dominion has become so pervasive as to coincide with the obvious. And this is its supreme triumph, as the supreme aspiration of the Devil is to convince everyone that he doesn't exist.

In a century as wracked by upheavals as was the nineteenth, the event that in fact summed up all the others was to pass unobserved: the pseudomorphism between religious and social. It all came together not so much in Durkheim's claim that "the religious is the social," but in the fact that suddenly such a claim *sounded natural.* And as the century grew old, it certainly wasn't religion that was conquering new territories, beyond liturgy and cult, as Victor Hugo and many who followed him imagined, but the social that was gradually invading and annexing vast tracts of the religious, first by superimposing itself on it, then by infiltrating it in an unhealthy amalgamation until finally it had incorporated the whole of the religious in itself. What was left in the end was naked society, but invested now with all the powers inherited, or rather burgled, from religion. The twentieth century would see its triumph. The theology of society severed every tie, renounced all dependence, and flaunted its distinguishing feature: the tautological, the self-advertising. The power and impact of totalitarian regimes cannot be explained unless we accept that the very notion of society has appropriated an unprecedented power, one previously the preserve of religion. The results were not long in coming: the liturgies in the stadiums, the positive heroes, the fecund women, the massacres. Being antisocial would become the equivalent of sinning against the Holy Ghost. Whether the pretexts spoke of race or class, the one sufficient reason for killing your enemies was always the same: these people were harmful to society. Society becomes the subject above all subjects, for whose sake everything is justified. At first with recourse to a grandiloquent rhetoric brutally wrenched from religion (the sacrifice *for* the fatherland), but later in the name of the mere functioning of society itself, which demands the removal of every obstacle.

For that hardly numerous and variously scattered sect who wouldn't have anything to do with this, mostly out of a purely physiological incompatibility, the only sign of mutual recognition left was "that very word literature, a word without honor, a belated arrival, useful above all for manuals," a word that stands out all the more, alone and unscathed, when "the genres break up and the forms melt away, when on the one hand the world has no more need for literature and on the other every book seems alien to all the others and indifferent to the reality of the genres." And here we are bound to acknowledge an extraordinary phenomenon: that to follow the chequered and tortuous history of absolute literature we will have to rely almost exclusively on the writers themselves. Certainly not on the historians, who have still to appreciate what has happened; and only rarely on those who are exclusively critics; while those other disciplines that claimed to have a role to play—semiology, for example—have turned out to be superfluous, or irksome. Only the writers are able to open up their secret laboratories for us. Capricious and elusive guides as they are, they are the only ones who know the territory well: when we read the essays of Baudelaire or Proust, of Hofmannsthal or Benn, Valéry or Auden, Brodsky or Mandelstam, Marina Tsvetayeva or Karl Kraus, Yeats or Montale, Borges or Nabokov, Manganelli, Calvino, Canetti, Kundera, we immediately sense— even though each may have hated, or ignored, or even opposed the other—that they are all *talking about the same thing*. Which doesn't mean they are eager to put a name to it. Protected by a variety of masks, they know that the literature they're talking about is not to be recognized by its observance of any theory, but rather by a certain vibration or luminescence of the sentence (or paragraph, or page, or chapter, or whole book even). This kind of literature is a creature that is sufficient unto itself. But that doesn't mean that it is merely self-referential, as a new species of bigots would have it. These new bigots are in fact a mirror image of the ingenuous realists, who were demolished in a single remark of Nabokov's when he spoke of the "reality" that can only be named between inverted commas. And on another occasion he observed how those commas dig their claws into it. There is no doubt of course that literature is self-referential: how can any form not be so? But at the same time it is omnivorous, like the stomachs of those animals that are found to contain nails, pot shards, and handkerchiefs— sometimes intact too, insolent reminders that something did happen down there, in that place made up of multiple, divergent, and poorly defined *realia*, which is the riverbed of all literature. But likewise of life in general.

We shall have to resign ourselves to this: that literature offers no signs, has never offered any signs, by which it can immediately be identified. The best, if not the only, test that we can apply is that suggested by Housman: check if a sequence of words, silently pronounced as the razor glides across our skin of a morning, sets the hairs of the beard on end, while a "shiver" goes "down the spine." Nor is this mere physiological reductionism. He who recalls a line of verse while shaving experiences that shiver, that *romaharṣa*, or "horripilation," that befalls Arjuna in the *Bhagavad Gītā* when overwhelmed by the epiphany of Kṛṣṇa. And perhaps *romaharṣa* would better be translated as "happiness of the hairs," because *harṣa* means "happiness," as well as "erection," including the sexual variety. This is typical of a language like Sanskrit that does not love the explicit, but hints that everything is sexual. As for Baudelaire, he was proud that Hugo had sensed, on reading his verses, a "new shiver." How else could we recognize poetry—and its departure from what came before? Something happens, something Coomaraswamy defined as "the aesthetic shock." Whether prompted by the apparition of a god or a sequence of words, the nature of that shock doesn't change. And this is what poetry does: it makes us see what otherwise we wouldn't have seen, through a sound that was never heard before.

But what did the writers I've mentioned mean when they said or thought of something, "It's literature"? Allergic to the idea of belonging to anything, honorable members, no less than Groucho Marx, of the club of those who would never join a club that accepted them as members, they used that word to refer to the only landscape where they felt alive: a sort of second reality that opens out beyond the cracks of that other reality where everyone has agreed on the conventions that make the world machine go round. That these cracks exist is itself a metaphysical proposition—and not all of these writers were interested in practicing philosophy. Yet that is how they behaved, as if literature were a sort of natural metaphysics, irrepressible, based not on a chain of concepts but rather on irregular entities—scraps of images, assonance, rhythms, gestures, forms of whatever kind. Perhaps this is the crucial word: "form." Repeated for centuries, for all kinds of reasons and in all kinds of guises, it still seems to be the base beneath all bases when one speaks of literature. An elusive base too, intrinsically incapable of being translated into some definition. For one can speak convincingly of form only by resorting to other forms. There is no language of a higher order than form which might explain it, or make it functional to something else—just as there is no language of a higher order than myth. Yet the notion that there is such a superordinate language has been the premise of entire disciplines and schools of thought that have swept over the world in swarm after swarm without ever so much as scratching the surface of what continues to be, in Goethe's words, the "open mystery" of every form.

Looking back at this long process, one asks oneself: when is it that its distinctive and unmistakable timbre is heard for the first time? When is it that, reading this page or that, we feel sure we have found a foretaste of the extraordinary story to come, still unaware of itself, yet at the same time unassimilable to any previous story? Reading the "Monologue" of Novalis perhaps:

In speaking and in writing something mad occurs: the true conversation is a pure play of words. What's amazing, in fact, is that people should make such a ridiculous mistake as to imagine they are speaking of things. Precisely what is most characteristic of language—that it attends only to itself—everybody ignores. As a result it is a wondrous and fruitful mystery—to the point that, if one speaks purely for the sake of speaking, one expresses the most splendid, the most original truths. But if a person wishes to speak of some particular thing, that capricious creature language has him say the most ridiculous and muddle-headed of stuff.

Which explains the hatred some serious people have for language. They see its mischievousness, but they don't see that contemptible chatter is the infinitely serious side of language. If only one could have people understand that what applies to mathematical formulas applies to language too. They form a world apart, they play with each other, expressing only their own prodigious nature, which is precisely why they are so expressive—precisely why the strange play of relationships between things finds its reflection in them. Only by means of their freedom are they members of nature, and only in their free movements does the spirit of the world manifest itself and make itself the delicate measure and pattern of things. The same is true of language: he who has a subtle sense of its fingering, its timing, its musical spirit, he who intuits the delicate operation of its intimate nature, moving tongue or hand to it as he follows, he will be a prophet; conversely, he who knows this, but does not have the ear or the ability to write truths like these, will be mocked by language itself and derided by men, as was Cassandra by the Trojans. If in saying this I believe I have shown, in the clearest way possible, the essence and office of poetry, all the same I know that no one will be able to understand me and I will have said something foolish precisely because I wanted to say it, so that no poetry has come out of it at all. But what if I felt compelled to speak? what if this linguistic impulse to speak were the hallmark of the inspiration of language, of the operation of language, in me? what if my will wanted only what I am compelled to do? might not this, in the end, without my realizing or imagining it, be poetry and make a mystery of language comprehensible? and would I then be a writer by vocation, since a writer can only be someone who is possessed by language?

Without equal either in the other writings of Novalis or indeed in Romantic literature in general, this page has to be quoted in full. It's not an argument, or a series of arguments, but a continuous flow of words about language, where one has the impression that it is the language itself that is speaking. Never before had language and reflection on language come so close together. They skim over each other without coinciding. And that they don't quite coincide is only a heightened pleasure added to the text, as if they might coincide at any moment, but instead leave open a tiny gap, to breathe through. Heidegger, who revered this text, nevertheless objected to the way it conceives language "dialectically, within the perspective of absolute idealism, on the basis of subjectivity." A specious objection: there is no trace of dialectical machinery in the "Monologue." Nor does one sense any need to resort to something called "subjectivity." What disturbed Heidegger here, one suspects, was something else altogether: the volatile, even flighty nature of the passage, its strenuous resistance to conceptualization, the effrontery with which it offers, as "contemptible chatter" about *chatter*, unfathomable speculations that take us as close as possible to the wellspring of the word. This is the characteristic gesture of absolute literature. And it is this that worries Heidegger; he senses it is uncontrollable, even with all his powerful strategic apparatus. In this passage, then, which bears no signature, an acephalous text, a sheet of paper mislaid perhaps, hard to date—though quite likely written in 1798, a year of important beginnings—in these few lines quickly whispered like some demonic *presto*, absolute literature presents itself in all its recklessness: irresponsible, metamorphic, carrying no identity card that a desk sergeant might examine, deceptive in its tone (so much so that some germanists bereft of irony would imagine that the "Monologue" itself was ironic in intent), and, finally, subject to no authority, whether it be venerable rhetoric or metaphysics, or even a system of thought like Heidegger's that claimed to be *beyond* metaphysics. Because committed only to its own elaboration, like a child playing alone, absorbed in his game. "Monological art," Gottfried Benn would one day call it, Benn who was himself to formulate the most corrosive and impudent version of this mutation of literature that the twentieth century would witness. Exhausted, his work still banned,

Berlin in ruins round his clinic for syphilitics, he wrote the following letter to Dieter Wellershoff:

> You speak of styles: the penetrating style, the lean style, the musical style, the intimate style—all excellent points of view, but don't forget: the expressive style, where the only thing that counts is the seduction and the imprint of the expression, where the contents are only euphorizations for artistic exercises . . . In this regard, take a look at the novels and verse of the second half of the nineteenth century. The period has good intentions, it is upright, sincere (in the old-fashioned sense), certainly not without its attractions, but it *depicts*, states of mind, relationships, situations, it transmits experiences and knowledge, but here the language is not the essential creative power, it is not itself. And then along comes Nietzsche and *the* language begins, and all it wants to do, all it can do, is phosphoresce, flash, ravish, amaze. It celebrates itself, it draws everything human into its slight but powerful organism, becomes monological, even monomaniacal. A tragic style, a crisis style, hybrid, final . . .

A hundred and fifty years on and from behind a heap of rubble it's as if the "Monologue" of Novalis were still going on. The tone is different now, of course. Abandoning the angelic, it inclines to the poisonous. But the voices are recognizably similar; they call to each other, twine together. Heidegger was right not to trust that page of Novalis. It announced a knowledge that refused to be subject to any other, and at the same time would seep into the cracks of all others. Literature grows like the grass between the heavy gray paving stones of thought. "And then along comes Nietzsche . . .": but why should such a drastic leap in the evolution of literature appear in the writings of a philosopher? Yet we feel Benn couldn't have chosen anyone else for the role. Why? Despite Heidegger's grandiose determination to demonstrate the contrary in two volumes and a thousand pages, Nietzsche was the first attempt to escape from a cage of categories whose origin we find in Plato and Aristotle. What may or may not lie beyond that cage has not yet been established. But many travelers have reported that literature is the passport most readily accepted in that terra incognita where—so one hears tell—all the mythologies now pass a largely indolent life in a no-man's-land haunted by gods and vagrant simulacra, by ghosts and Gypsy caravans in constant movement. All these beings are ever issuing from the cave of the past. They yearn only to tell their stories again, as the shades of the underworld yearned only for blood. But how can we reach them? Culture, in the most recent sense of the word, should imply the ability to celebrate, invisibly, the rites that open the way to this kingdom, which is also the kingdom of the dead. Yet it is precisely this ability that is so obviously lacking in the world around us. Behind the trembling curtains of what passes for "reality," the voices throng. If no one listens, they steal the costume of the first person they can grab and burst onto the stage in ways that can be devastating. Violence is the expedient of whatever has been refused an audience.

This is the country that Nietzsche set out to explore, the country that swallowed him up. The country of "truth and untruth in an extra-moral sense," as he put it in the title of a brief text that dates back to the period of *The Birth of Tragedy* and shares with it its farsightedness and white heat, albeit with a different stylistic gesture—deft, light, digressive, as if the healthier Nietzsche of *The Gay Science* were here making his first outing. But from the opening lines it's clear that what is to be at stake in these pages is nothing less than everything. At once Nietzsche sets out to tell us a story that has to do with a single minute in the history of the cosmos: "In a remote corner of the sparkling universe that stretches away across infinite solar systems, there was once a star where some clever animals invented knowledge. It was the most arrogant and deceitful minute in the 'history of the world': but it lasted only a minute. Nature breathed in and out just a few times, then the star hardened and the clever animals had to die." The crucial point in this fable comes when it says that knowledge is something *invented*. If one doesn't discover knowledge, but invents it, the implication is that it involves a powerful element of simulation. And Nietzsche goes so far as to claim that it is precisely in simulation that "the intellect unleashes its principal strengths." This would already be enough to undermine every previous edifice of knowledge. But with sovereign dispatch Nietzsche goes straight to the consequences and in just a few lines is posing the ultimate question: "What is the truth? A mobile army of metaphors." That does it. All at once "the huge scaffolding and support structures of the concepts" collapse: metaphor no longer signifies an ornament that doesn't bind, something only acceptable in the inconsistent world of the poets. On the contrary: if "man's fundamental instinct" is precisely "the instinct to form metaphors," and if concepts are no more or less than bleached and ossified metaphors, worn-out coinage, as Nietzsche dared to claim, then this instinct that is not placated in the "columbarium of concepts" will seek "another channel to flow in." Where? "In *myth*, and in general in *art*." With one quick thrust Nietzsche has attributed to art a supreme gnoseological quality. Knowledge and simulation are no longer enemies but accomplices. And if every kind of knowledge is a form of simulation, art is if nothing else the most immediate and the most vibrant. What's more: if metaphor is the normal and primordial vehicle of knowledge, then man's relationship with the gods and their myths will appear as something obvious and self-evident: "When once every tree can speak as a Nymph or when a god in the form of a bull can carry off a virgin, when the goddess Athena herself is to be seen beside Pisistratus crossing Athens on a fine chariot—and the honest Athenian believed as much—then, as in a dream, everything is possible at any moment, and all nature swarms around man, as though no less than the masquerade of the gods who play at deceiving us by taking on all sorts of shapes." Here, more than anywhere else, Nietzsche is wielding the "magic of the extreme," his greatest and most reckless virtue. So one might imagine that he had been left in glorious isolation, the only one to have situated the workings of art on such a tall gnoseological pinnacle. But not long after him we find the young Proust approaching the same position. Often depicted as a fatuous snob waiting to be struck by literary revelation, Proust actually looks forward to that revelation as something inevitable even before taking his first steps in society. And no sooner does he speak of literature and what it is than we note a certain toughness, an intransigence in his voice. Immediately he speaks about it in terms of *knowledge*.

Few words chime with more obsessive regularity in the *Recherche* than the word "laws," and this every time that appearances are torn open and a dark or dazzling background is glimpsed beyond. One is tempted to say that Proust's main concern was establishing laws, as if—rather than a novelist—it were a physicist writing. And this isn't a gambit he uses only in the *Recherche*, as a sort of personal gnoseological seal. In a fragment we can date back to the period of *Jean Santeuil*, and hence to a time of apparent worldly indulgence, Proust gives us, almost in passing, a definition of literature that goes so far as to have it coincide with its lawmaking function, beginning with the vision of the poet who "stands still before whatever does not deserve the attention of the sedate man, so much so that one wonders whether he might be a lover or a spy, or again, after it seems he's been looking at a tree for a long time, what in reality he is looking at." At this point one asks oneself, as in some Zen story, what there might be "beyond the tree." And here Proust offers us one of his wonderfully undulatory sentences and, set right in the middle, the formula we were looking for:

But the poet, who cheerfully senses the beauty of all things once he has gathered it into the mysterious laws he carries about within him, and who will soon have us rediscovering it in his charm, showing it to us through a hem of those mysterious laws, that hem that joins with them, that hem that he will also depict at the same time as he depicts things themselves, in touching their feet or starting from their brow, the poet feels and causes us cheerfully to know the beauty of all things, of a glass of water no less than of diamonds, but also of diamonds no less than of a glass of water, of a field as much as of a statue, but also of a statue as much as of a field.

It is not feelings, then, but laws that we find at the center of that perception which distinguishes the writer from every other being—and that causes him to observe the things of the world with the maniacal concentration that has us thinking of spies and lovers. The whole of the *Recherche* was to be woven out of these "mysterious laws" (which in the meantime had lost their adjective), but it seems clear that as far as Proust was concerned all literature must be woven from them. So much so that in the same text we find him using these laws to suggest a biological-metaphysical explanation of the *work*:

The poet's mind is full of manifestations of the mysterious laws and, when these manifestations appear, they grow more vigorous, they detach themselves vigorously on the mind's deep bed, they aspire to come out from him, because everything that must last aspires to come out from everything that is fragile, short-lived, and that could perish the very same evening or no longer be able to bring them to the light. So at every moment, whenever it feels strong enough and has an outlet, the human species tends to come out from itself, in a complete sperm, that contains the whole of it, of today's man who may die as we said this very evening, or who perhaps will no longer contain it in its wholeness, or in whom (since it depends on him so long as it is his prisoner) it will never be so strong again. Thus the thought of the mysterious laws, or poetry, when it feels strong enough, aspires to come out from the short-lived man who perhaps this evening will be dead or in whom (since it depends on him so long as it is his prisoner, and he could get sick, or be distracted, or grow worldly, less strong, squander in pleasure the treasure he carries within him and that decays if he chooses to live in a certain way, since its destiny is still tied to him) it will no longer have that mysterious energy that allows it to open out in its fullness, it aspires to come out from the man in the form of the work.

Behind the mixture, here particularly crude, of positivist physiology and Platonism—a mixture typical of Proust—we sense that something unchanging and essential has crystallized in these convoluted lines: above all the idea of poetry as "thought of the mysterious laws," while the work's necessity is seen as the transmigration of an immortal body that uses the writer's body as a temporary shell only to abandon it as soon as possible for fear of being suffocated. The following hypothesis thus presents itself: that it is precisely this process of osmotic transmission, from one work to the next, that, whenever the rash gesture that is absolute literature begins to take shape, renders every other connotation, whether of school, national tradition, or historical moment, inconsistent and secondary. The writers who in some way engage in that bold gesture will thus tend to form a sort of communion of saints, where the same fluid circulates from work to work, page to page, and each calls to the other from an affinity that is far stronger than any that might tie them to their time, or to some trend—or even to their own physiology and taste. This too is the "mystery in Literature" that declares itself, in its blazing obscurity, from the years of the *Athenaeum* review on—and which is still with us today, if only we care to notice. Any direct relationship is superfluous. But the affinity and the element of consequence between one link in the chain and the next make themselves felt most powerfully, as if in some renewed *aurea catena Homeri.*

The best analogy might be that of two mathematicians who, though unaware of each other and working thousands of miles apart, both feel an urgent need to solve some particular equation, something their colleagues pass by without even being aware of. One day the two mathematicians' notes may be juxtaposed, superimposed, to the point that we might think they were written by the same person, were it not for some different manner of procedure or exposition, since in the end each person always bears a trace of the "mysterious being we are, who possessed that gift of giving to everything a certain form that belongs only to ourselves." And if one day the mathematicians' paths should cross, they may well walk by each other without a word, like those priests of the god Hölderlin speaks of "who moved from country to country through the holy night."

We began with Homer; we have ended in a place that is the Elsewhere of every other. In between lies a path that is a weave of variants. Yet we know that behind every movement and tremor, the scene is always the same. It greets us from an Attic cup that dates back to the Wars of the Peloponnese and is now in Corpus Christi College, Cambridge. Three figures: To the left, sitting on a rock, a young man writes on a tablet, a *díptychon*, that looks very like a laptop. From beneath, a severed head watches as he writes. To the right, standing up, is Apollo: one hand grasps a laurel rod, while the other stretches out towards the young man writing.

What is going on? The way it is most frequently represented, Orpheus had his throat cut by a Maenad who held his hair tight from behind while plunging a sword into his neck. To defend himself, the poet brandished his lyre like a weapon, and sang. But the *vis carminum* could do no more than briefly hold back, suspended in the air, the stones hurled at him by other Maenads. Then a clash of arms drowned his voice and it could charm no longer. His head was cut off with a sickle. Tossed into the river Evros, it drifted with the current. Singing and bleeding. It was ever fresh, ever flourishing. It reached the sea, crossed a vast tract of the Aegean, and was washed up on Lesbos. Here, we presume, the scene depicted on the Attic *kýlix* took place. It is the primordial scene of all literature, composed of its irreducible elements.

Literature is never the product of a single subject. There are always at least three actors: the hand that writes, the voice that speaks, the god who watches over and compels. Not that they look very different: all three are young; all have thick, snaky hair. They might easily be taken for three manifestations of the same person. But that is hardly the point. What matters is the division into three self-sufficient beings. We could call them the I, the Self, and the Divine. A continuous process of triangulation is at work between them. Every sentence, every form, is a variation within that force field. Hence the ambiguity of literature: because its point of view is incessantly shifting between these three extremes, without warning us, and sometimes without warning the author. The young man writing is absorbed at his tablet; it's as if he didn't see anything of what is around him. And perhaps he doesn't. Perhaps he has no idea who is beside him. The stylus that etches the letters demands all his attention. The head that drifts on the waters sings and bleeds. Every vibration of the word presupposes something violent, a *palaiòn pénthos*, an "ancient grief." Was it a murder? Was it a sacrifice? It isn't clear, but the word will never cease to tell of it. Apollo grasps his laurel rod, his other arm stretching out to hint at something. Is he compelling? forbidding? protecting? We will never know. But that outstretched arm, like the arm of the Apollo of the Master of Olympia, a motionless axis in the center of a vortex, invests and sustains the whole scene—and all literature.

SOURCES

The first number in the left column
refers to the page, the second to the
line on which the quotation ends.

I

4,17   *Iliad*, XIII, 71.

5,2   *Odyssey*, XIII, 112.

5,3   *Hymn to Demeter*, III.

5,8   *Odyssey*, XVI, 61.

5,23   Euripides, *Helen*, 560.

5,25   K. Kerényi, *Antike Religion*, Klett-Cotta, Stuttgart, 1995, p. 160.

6,7   Aratus, *Phaenomena*, 1–5.

6,8   Virgil, *Eclogues*, III, 60.

6,28   Ch. Baudelaire, "L'École païenne," in *Œuvres complètes*, ed. C. Pichois, Gallimard, Paris, vol. II, 1976, p. 44.

7,8   *Loc. cit.*

7,11   *Loc. cit.*

8,10   *Ibid.*, pp. 44–45.

8,17   *Ibid.*, p. 45.

9,25   Madame de Staël, *De l'Allemagne*, Garnier-Flammarion, Paris, 1968, vol. I, p. 51.

10,6   *Ibid.*, p. 55.

10,14   F. Hölderlin, letter no. 240 to C. U. Böhlendorff, in *Briefe*, ed. F. Beissner, Kohlhammer, Stuttgart, 1959, p. 462.

10,18   *Loc. cit.*

11,22   Ch. Baudelaire, "L'École païenne," cit., p. 45.

11,27   Ch. Baudelaire, "Exposition universelle—1855—Beaux-Arts," in *Œuvres complètes*, cit., vol. II, p. 577.

12,1   Ch. Baudelaire, "Lettre à Jules Janin," in *Œuvres complètes*, cit., vol. II, p. 233.

12,4   *Ibid.*, p. 232.

12,8   Ch. Baudelaire, *Correspondance*, ed. C. Pichois, Gallimard,

Paris, 1973, vol. II,
p. 471.

12,14 Ch. Baudelaire,
"Lettre à Jules Janin,"
cit., p. 233.

12,16 *Ibid.*, p. 232.

13,14 Ch. Baudelaire,
"L'École païenne,"
cit., p. 46.

14,9 H. Heine,
Elementargeister, in
Sämtliche Schriften,
ed. K. Briegleb,
Hanser, Munich, 1978,
vol. III, p. 686.

14,23 H. Heine,
Elementargeister,
second French
version, in *Sämtliche
Schriften*, cit., vol. III,
p. 1024.

17,23 Ch. Baudelaire,
"L'École païenne," cit.
pp. 47–49.

19,6 P. Verlaine, "Les
Dieux," ll. 1–4.

19,12 *Loc. cit.*

19,14 *Loc. cit.*

19,15 *Loc. cit.*

19,22 *Loc. cit.*

21,1 F. Nietzsche,
*Nachgelassene
Fragmente (Herbst
1887 bis März 1888)*, in
Werke, ed. G. Colli
and M. Montinari, De
Gruyter, Berlin–New

York, vol. VIII/2,
1970, p. 176.

II

27,3 A. Warburg,
"Burckhardt-
Übungen," in E. H.
Gombrich, *Aby
Warburg*, Phaidon,
Oxford, 1986, p. 254.

28,8 F. Nietzsche, letter to
Jacob Burckhardt, 4
January 1889, in
Briefwechsel, ed. G.
Colli and M.
Montinari, De
Gruyter, Berlin–
NewYork, vol. III/5,
1984, p. 574.

30,10 A. Warburg, *Sandro
Botticellis «Geburt
der Venus» und
'Frühling'*, in
Gesammelte Schriften,
B. G. Teubner,
Leipzig–Berlin, 1932,
vol. I, p. 20.

30,21 *Hymn to Apollo*,
244.

30,25 *Ibid.*, 251.

31,2 *Ibid.*, 300, 376.

31,25 Plato, *Phaedrus*,
238 d.

32,2 Apollonius Rhodius,
Argonautica, I,
1238–1239.

32,7 Porphyry, *The Cave of the Nymphs*, 8.

33,8 V. Nabokov, *Lolita*, Putnam, New York, 1958, p. 18.

33,15 *Ibid.*, p. 141.

34,2 E. Pound, *Guide to Kulchur*, New Directions, New York, 1970, p. 299.

34,7 V. Nabokov, *Lolita*, cit., p. 131.

35,8 W. Michel, *Das Leben Friedrich Hölderlins*, Schünemann, Bremen, 1940, p. 261.

35,18 F. Hölderlin, letter no. 236 to C. U. Böhlendorff, in *Briefe*, cit., p. 456.

36,6 F. Schiller, letter to J. G. Herder, 4 November 1795, in *Briefe*, ed. G. Fricke, Hanser, Munich, 1955, p. 375.

36,20 G. Leopardi, *Zibaldone*, ed. R. Damiani, Mondadori, Milano, 1997, vol. II, p. 1856.

36,24 *Ibid.*, vol. I, p. 288.

37,2 *Ibid.*, p. 289.

37,7 *Ibid.*, vol. II, p. 2157.

37,10 *Ibid.*, p. 2158.

37,11 *Loc. cit.*

37,13 *Loc. cit.*

37,27 *Ibid.*, p. 1857.

38,18 *Ibid.*, p. 1858.

39,4 F. Hölderlin, "Das Höchste," in *Sämtliche Werke*, ed. F. Beissner, Insel, Frankfurt a. M., 1961, p. 1256.

39,18 *Loc. cit.*

39,19 F. Hölderlin, "Wie wenn am Feiertage . . . ," ll. 22, 25.

39,21 M. Heidegger, *Erläuterungen zu Hölderlins Dichtung*, Klostermann, Frankfurt a. M., 1963, p. 61.

40,2 *Loc. cit.*

40,9 *Ibid.*, p. 62.

40,11 *Loc. cit.*

40,16 R. M. Rilke, *Duineser Elegien*, I, ll. 4–5.

41,13 F. Hölderlin, "Wie wenn am Feiertage . . . ," l. 20.

41,15 *Ibid.*, l. 23.

42,2 F. Schlegel, "Rede über die Mythologie," from *Gespräch über die Poesie*, in *Kritische Ausgabe*, vol. II: *Charakteristiken und Kritiken I*, ed. H. Eichner,

Schöningh, Munich, 1967, p. 319.

42,3 *Loc. cit.*

42,5 *Loc. cit.*

42,25 F. Hölderlin, "Patmos," ll. 1–2.

43,25 Apollonius Rhodius, *Argonautica*, II, 669–684.

44,7 *Ibid.*, II, 686–688.

44,19 F. Hölderlin, letter no. 236 to C. U. Böhlendorff, in *Briefe*, cit., p. 456.

44,23 *Loc. cit.*

44,25 *Loc. cit.*

45,16 F. Hölderlin, "Anmerkungen zum Oedipus," in *Sämtliche Werke*, cit., p. 1188.

45,23 *Loc. cit.*

45,27 *Loc. cit.*

46,17 F. Hölderlin, "Der Gesichtspunkt, aus dem wir das Altertum anzusehen haben," in *Sämtliche Werke*, cit., p. 950.

46,25 *Ibid.*, pp. 950–951.

47,2 F. Hölderlin, "Mnemosyne," second draft, ll. 2–3.

47,12 F. Hölderlin, letter no. 236 to C. U. Böhlendorff, in *Briefe*, cit., p. 456.

47,15 *Loc. cit.*

47,26 H. Vaughan, "The World," ll. 1–3.

48,16 F. Hölderlin, "Der Vatikan," l. 12.

48,27 F. Hölderlin, "Griechenland," l. 1.

48,27 F. Hölderlin, "Der Frühling," l. 2.

49,6 F. Hölderlin, "Komet," in *144 fliegende Briefe*, ed. D. E. Sattler, Luchterhand, Darmstadt, 1981, vol. II, p. 351.

III

54,25 I. Calvino, *Saggi 1945–1985*, Mondadori, Milano, 1995, vol. I, p. 1018.

56,2 *Atharva Veda*, 12, 1, 13.

56,6 *Ibid.*, 12, 1, 21.

56,10 *Ibid.*, 12, 1, 24.

56,12 *Ibid.*, 12, 1, 57.

56,15 *Ibid.*, 12, 1, 26.

57,22 ["Das älteste Systemprogramm des deutschen Idealismus"], in G.W.F. Hegel, *Werke*, Suhrkamp, Frankfurt a. M., vol. I, 1971, p. 236.

57,27 *Loc. cit.*

58,7 F. Nietzsche, *Die Geburt der Tragödie*, in *Werke*, cit., vol. III/1, 1972, p. 141.

58,16 F. Schlegel, "Rede über die Mythologie," cit., p. 312.

59,3 *Loc. cit.*

59,13 *Ibid.*, p. 313.

60,7 *Ibid.*, p. 319.

60,8 *Ibid.*, pp. 319–320.

61,8 F. Schlegel, *Über die Sprache und Weisheit der Indier*, Mohr, Heidelbergae, 1808, p. 91.

62,23 Plato, *Phaedrus*, 244 d.

63,8 F. Hölderlin, "Brot und Wein," l. 54.

63,11 *Ibid.*, l. 108.

63,17 *Ibid.*, ll. 113–114.

64,8 F. Creuzer, *Dionysus*, Mohr, Heidelbergae, 1808, p. 1.

64,13 *Ibid.*, p. 5.

64,26 Heraclitus, fr. A 60 (Colli).

65,19 Aristotle, *On Philosophy*, fr. 15 (Ross).

66,9 F. Nietzsche, *Nachgelassene Fragmente (Herbst 1869 bis Herbst 1872)*, in *Werke*, cit., vol. III/3, 1978, p. 213.

66,26 *Ibid.*, p. 320.

66,27 *Ibid.*, p. 392.

67,3 *Ibid.*, p. 315.

67,7 F. Nietzsche, *Die Geburt der Tragödie*, cit., p. 123.

67,20 *Ibid.*, p. 145.

68,7 F. Nietzsche, *Nachgelassene Fragmente (Herbst 1869 bis Herbst 1872)*, cit., p. 273.

68,8 *Ibid.*, p. 310.

68,11 *Loc. cit.*

68,18 *Ibid.*, p. 253.

68,26 *Ibid.*, p. 166.

69,6 *Loc. cit.*

69,16 F. Nietzsche, letter to Carl von Gersdorff, 21 June 1871, in *Briefwechsel*, cit., vol. II/1, 1977, p. 204.

70,1 F. Nietzsche, *Die fröhliche Wissenschaft*, in *Werke*, cit., vol. V/2, 1973, p. 310.

70,15 F. Nietzsche, *Nachgelassene Fragmente (Herbst 1869 bis Herbst 1872)*, cit., p. 297.

70,18 *Ibid.*, p. 254.

70,24 F. Nietzsche, *Die Geburt der Tragödie*, cit., p. 16.

72,19 F. Nietzsche, "Wie die 'wahre Welt' endlich zur Fabel wurde," in *Götzen-Dämmerung*, in *Werke*, cit., vol. VI/3, 1969, pp. 74–75.

73,29 F. Nietzsche, *Nachgelassene Fragmente (Anfang 1888 bis Anfang Januar 1889)*, in *Werke*, cit., vol. VIII/3, 1972, p. 323.

74,3 F. Nietzsche, *Also sprach Zarathustra*, in *Werke*, cit., vol. VI/1, 1968, p. 244.

74,18 F. Nietzsche, *Die fröhliche Wissenschaft*, cit., p. 319.

74,24 *Loc. cit.*

74,28 *Ibid.*, p. 14.

75,13 F. Nietzsche, letter to Jacob Burckhardt, 6 January 1889, in *Briefwechsel*, cit., vol. III/5, 1984, pp. 577–578.

IV

80,2 Lautréamont, letter to Monsieur Darasse, 12 March 1870, in *Œuvres complètes*, ed. P.-O. Walzer, Gallimard, Paris, 1970, p. 301.

80,10 Lautréamont, *Poésies I*, in *Œuvres complètes*, ed. Walzer, cit., p. 265.

81,7 *Ibid.*, p. 267.

81,19 Lautréamont, *Les Chants de Maldoror*, in *Œuvres complètes*, ed. Walzer, cit., p. 139.

81,23 *Loc. cit.*

81,25 *Ibid.*, p. 140.

81,27 *Loc. cit.*

82,1 *Loc. cit.*

82,10 J. Gracq, "Lautréamont toujours," in Lautréamont, *Œuvres complètes*, Corti, Paris, 1958, p. 82.

83,7 M. Blanchot, *Faux pas*, Gallimard, Paris, 1975, p. 198.

83,9 B. Fondane, *Rimbaud le voyou*, Denoël, Paris, 1933, p. 190.

83,19 Lautréamont, *Les Chants de Maldoror*, cit., pp. 85, 87.

83,21 *Ibid.*, pp. 93, 95.

83,23 *Ibid.*, pp. 136, 137.

83,27 *Ibid.*, pp. 128, 129.

84,6 *Ibid.*, p. 183.

85,4 Novalis, "Die Christenheit oder Europa," in *Schriften*,

ed. R. Samuel, H.-J.
Mähl and G. Schulz,
Kohlhammer,
Stuttgart, vol. III,
1983, p. 520.

86,9 Lautréamont, letter to
Poulet-Malassis (some
claim it was addressed
to Monsieur
Verboeckhoven), 23
October 1869, in
Œuvres complètes, ed.
Walzer, cit., p. 296.

86,16 Quoted in J.-J.
Lefrère, *Isidore
Ducasse*, Fayard,
Paris, 1998, p. 445.

86,26 Lautréamont, letter to
Poulet-Malassis, 23
October 1869, in
Œuvres complètes, ed.
Walzer, cit., p. 296.

87,12 Quoted in J.-J.
Lefrère, *Isidore
Ducasse*, cit., p. 449.

87,23 Lautréamont, *Les
Chants de Maldoror*,
cit., p. 122.

88,8 Lautréamont, letter to
Poulet-Malassis, 23
October 1869, in
Œuvres complètes, ed.
Walzer, cit., p. 297.

88,26 Lautréamont, letter to
Poulet-Malassis, 21
February 1870, *ibid.*,
p. 298.

89,14 *Loc. cit.*

91,17 Lautréamont, letter to
Monsieur Darasse, 12
March 1870, *ibid.*, p.
301.

91,23 Lautréamont, letter to
Monsieur Darasse, 22
May 1869, *ibid.*, p.
296.

92,16 A. Artaud, "Lettre sur
Lautréamont," from
*Suppôts et
supplications*, in
Œuvres complètes,
Gallimard, Paris, vol.
XIV /7, 1978, p. 32.

92,22 Lautréamont,
Poésies I, cit.,
p. 262.

93,3 *Ibid.*, p. 265.

93,15 *Ibid.*, p. 259.

93,23 *Ibid.*, p. 260.

94,2 Lautréamont, *Les
Chants de Maldoror*,
cit., p. 234.

94,8 Lautréamont, *Poésies
I*, cit., p. 261.

94,21 *Ibid.*, p. 268.

95,26 B. Pascal, *Les
'Pensées' de Port-
Royal*, in *Œuvres
complètes*, ed. M. Le
Guern, Gallimard,
Paris, 2000, vol. II, p.
997.

96,6 Lautréamont, *Poésies
II*, in *Œuvres

complètes, ed. Walzer, cit., p. 288.

96,22   Ibid., p. 291.

97,7   La Bruyère, Des Ouvrages de l'esprit, in Les Caractères.

97,13   Lautréamont, Poésies II, cit., p. 292.

97,25   Ibid., p. 290.

98,10   Lautréamont, Les Chants de Maldoror, cit., p. 197.

98,15   Loc. cit.

98,18   Loc. cit.

98,20   Loc. cit.

98,23   R. de Gourmont, Introduction, in Lautréamont, Œuvres complètes, Corti, cit., p. 20.

99,12   Lautréamont, Poésies I, cit., p. 269.

99,15   J. Gracq, "Lautréamont toujours," cit., p. 81.

99,19   L. Bloy, Le Désespéré, Mercure de France, Paris, 1918, p. 39.

V

104,1   S. Mallarmé, letter to Paul Verlaine, 16 November 1885, in Œuvres complètes,

ed. B. Marchal, Gallimard, Paris, vol. I, 1998, p. 789.

104,2   S. Mallarmé, Les Dieux antiques, Gallimard, Paris, 1925, p. XII.

104,11   Ibid., p. 54.

104,27   G. W. Cox, A Manual of Mythology, Longman, London, 1867, p. 14.

105,7   B. Marchal, La Religion de Mallarmé, Corti, Paris, 1988, pp. 147–148.

106,11   G. W. Cox, A Manual of Mythology, cit., p. 14.

106,14   S. Mallarmé, Les Dieux antiques, cit., p. 54.

107,12   S. Mallarmé, "Le Mystère dans les lettres," in Divagations, Charpentier, Paris, 1897, p. 284.

107,17   S. Mallarmé, letter to H. Cazalis, 14 May 1867, in Correspondance 1862–1871, ed. H. Mondor, Gallimard, Paris, 1959, p. 241.

107,21 Loc. cit.

107,28 Lautréamont, *Les
Chants de Maldoror*,
cit., p. 126.

108,15 S. Mallarmé, letter to
Th. Aubanel, 28 July
1866, in
*Correspondance
1862–1871*, cit., pp.
224–225.

109,8 *Bṛhadāraṇyaka
Upaniṣad*, 2, 1, 20.

109,12 *Śvetāśvatara
Upaniṣad*, 6, 10.

109,16 *Muṇḍaka Upaniṣad*,
1, 1, 7.

109,21 S. Mallarmé, letter to
H. Cazalis, 28 April
1866, in
*Correspondance
1862–1871*, cit., p. 207.

110,8 S. Mallarmé, letter to
H. Cazalis, 14 May
1867, *ibid.*, p. 243.

110,14 S. Mallarmé, letter to
H. Cazalis, 3 June
1863, *ibid.*, p. 91.

110,25 S. Mallarmé, letter to
H. Cazalis, 28 April
1866, *ibid.*, p. 207.

110,26 Loc. cit.

111,10 *Ibid.*, pp. 207–208.

112,2 S. Mallarmé, letter to
H. Cazalis, 13 July
1866, *ibid.*,
p. 220.

112,4 S. Mallarmé, letter to
H. Cazalis, 14 May
1867, *ibid.*, p. 244.

112,8 S. Mallarmé, letter to
A. Renaud, 28
December 1866, in
Œuvres complètes, ed.
Marchal, cit., vol. I, p.
712.

112,9 S. Mallarmé, letter to
H. Cazalis, 14 May
1867, in
*Correspondance
1862–1871*, cit., p. 243.

112,26 S. Mallarmé, letter to
E. Lefébure, 17 May
1867, *ibid.*, pp.
249–250.

114,7 S. Mallarmé, letter to
E. Lefébure, 27 May
1867, *ibid.*, p. 246.

114,1 S. Mallarmé, letter
to H. Cazalis,
14 May 1867, *ibid.*,
p. 241.

114,21 *Ibid.*, p. 242.

115,7 *Taittirīya Saṃhitā*, 2,
5, 11, 15.

115,8 *Śatapatha
Brāhmaṇa*, 4, 1, 1, 22.

115,23 M. Proust, letter to
Reynaldo Hahn, 28
August 1896, in
Correspondance, ed.
Ph. Kolb, Plon, Paris,
vol. II, 1976, p. 111.

117,9 S. Mallarmé, "Sonnet allégorique de lui-même," in *Œuvres complètes*, ed. Marchal, cit., vol. I, p. 131.

118,7 S. Mallarmé, letter to H. Cazalis, 18 July 1868, in *Correspondance 1862–1871*, cit., p. 278.

118,12 S. Mallarmé, letter to F. Coppée, 5 December 1866, *ibid.*, p. 234.

118,22 S. Mallarmé, letter to H. Cazalis, 18 July 1868, *ibid.*, p. 279.

119,9 *Loc. cit.*

120,15 *Ibid.*, p. 278.

120,17 Translation by J.-M. Durand, in *Archives épistolaires de Mari*, Recherche sur les civilisations, Paris, 1998, vol. I/1, p. 478.

121,27 S. Mallarmé, letter to H. Cazalis, 14 May 1867, in *Correspondance 1862–1871*, cit., pp. 241–242.

122,6 *Loc. cit.*

122,11 S. Mallarmé, "Sonnet allégorique de lui-même," l. 14.

VI

125,5 S. Mallarmé, letter to Marie and Geneviève Mallarmé, 1 March 1894, in *Correspondance*, ed. H. Mondor and L. J. Austin, Gallimard, Paris, vol. VI, 1981, p. 233.

125,8 S. Mallarmé, "La Musique et les Lettres," in *Œuvres complètes*, ed. H. Mondor and G. Jean-Aubry, Gallimard, Paris, 1956, p. 643.

125,14 *Loc. cit.*

126,5 *Ibid.*, pp. 643–644.

126,9 *Ibid.*, p. 644.

126,12 *Loc. cit.*

126,14 *Loc. cit.*

127,27 S. Mallarmé, "Crise de vers," in *Divagations*, cit., pp. 236–237.

128,20 *Ibid.*, p. 240.

128,23 *Ibid.*, p. 248.

128,25 *Ibid.*, p. 239.

129,1 *Loc. cit.*

129,10 *Loc. cit.*

129,23 S. Mallarmé, "Sur l'évolution littéraire," in *Œuvres complètes*, ed. Mondor and Jean-Aubry, cit., p. 867.

130,13 S. Mallarmé, "Crise de vers," cit., p. 248.

130,24 S. Mallarmé, "Sur l'évolution littéraire," cit., p. 866.

130,27 *Ibid.*, p. 867.

131,22 Ch. Baudelaire, *Le Spleen de Paris*, in *Œuvres complètes*, cit., vol. I, 1975, p. 303.

132,9 Ch. Baudelaire, "L'invitation au voyage," ll. 15–17.

132,17 Ch. Baudelaire, *Le Spleen de Paris*, cit., p. 302.

133,4 Ch. Baudelaire, "L'Invitation au voyage," l. 1.

133,6 Ch. Baudelaire, *Le Spleen de Paris*, cit., p. 301.

133,9 *Loc. cit.*

133,10 *Ibid.*, p. 302.

133,14 *Ibid.*, p. 303.

133,18 *Loc. cit.*

133,20 Ch. Baudelaire, "L'Invitation au voyage," l. 22.

134,25 P. Verlaine, "Art poétique," l. 17.

135,4 Ch. Baudelaire, *Le Spleen de Paris*, cit., p. 275.

135,15 *Loc. cit.*

135,21 G. Contini, "Sans rythme," in *Ultimi esercizî ed elzeviri*, Einaudi, Torino, 1988, p. 24.

135,23 Ch. Baudelaire, *Le Spleen de Paris*, cit., p. 278.

135,25 G. Contini, "Sans rythme," cit. p. 25.

135,28 *Loc. cit.*

136,9 *Ibid.*, p. 30.

136,20 *Ibid.*, p. 26.

137,7 Ch. Baudelaire, "Le Poison," 7.

138,2 S. Mallarmé, "Crise de vers," cit., p. 236.

138,5 *Loc. cit.*

138,10 *Loc. cit.*

138,20 W. B. Yeats, *Autobiographies*, Macmillan, London, 1961, p. 349.

139,3 S. Mallarmé, "Crise de vers," cit., p. 240.

139,6 *Ibid.*, pp. 240–241.

139,12 *Ibid.*, p. 239.

139,24 S. Mallarmé, "Le Mystère dans les Lettres," cit., p. 284.

140,5 S. Mallarmé, "Crise de vers," cit., p. 240.

140,9 *Ibid.*, p. 241.

140,13 *Loc. cit.*

140,16 *Ibid.*, p. 250.

140,24   S. Mallarmé, "La
Musique et les
Lettres," cit., p. 646.

140,27   *L'Amitié de Stéphane
Mallarmé et de
Georges Rodenbach*,
Cailler, Genève, 1949,
p. 141.

VII

145,1   *Śatapatha
Brāhmaṇa*, 4, 4, 3, 1.

145,17   *Ibid.*, 10, 4, 4, 1.

146,3   *Taittirīya Saṃhitā*, 5,
6, 6, 1.

146,9   *Śatapatha
Brāhmaṇa*, 7, 2, 1, 4;
7, 3, 2, 6.

147,2   *Ibid.*, 2, 3, 1, 17.

147,14   *Ibid.*, 1, 4, 4, 7.

147,27   *Loc. cit.*

148,14   *Ṛgveda*, 10, 125, 8.

148,27   *Śatapatha
Brāhmaṇa*, 8, 2, 2, 8.

149,4   *Ibid.*, 1, 8, 2, 8.

150,1   *Ibid.*, 3, 4, 1, 7.

150,4   *Ibid.*, 3, 3, 4, 7.

150,17   *Ibid.*, 4, 3, 2, 5.

151,6   M. Bloomfield, review
of W. Neisser, *Zum
Wörterbuch des
Ṛgveda*, in "Journal of
the American Oriental
Society," XLV, 1925,
p. 159.

152,26   L. Renou, *Études
védiques et
pāṇinéennes*, de
Boccard, Paris, vol. I,
1980, p. 15.

153,2   *Ibid.*, p. 26.

153,4   *Loc. cit.*

153,18   S. Mallarmé, "Crise de
vers," cit., p. 250.

153,22   *Jaiminīya Upaniṣad
Brāhmaṇa*, 1, 1, 1, 5.

154,11   *Śatapatha
Brāhmaṇa*, 10,
4, 1, 16.

155,6   M. Mayrhofer,
*Etymologisches
Wörterbuch des
Altindoarischen*,
Winter, Heidelberg,
vol. I/6, 1989, p. 429.

155,24   *Bṛhadāraṇyaka
Upaniṣad*, 3, 6, 1.

156,2   *Ibid.*, 3, 8, 3.

156,14   *Ibid.*, 3, 8, 7–8.

156,22   *Ṛgveda*, 3, 55, 1.

157,2   *Chāndogya
Upaniṣad*, 3, 12, 1.

157,9   *Ṛgveda*, 1, 164, 41–42.

158,1   J.A.B. van Buitenen,
Akṣara, in "Journal
of the American
Oriental Society,"
LXXXIX, 1959, p. 178.

158,8   *Śatapatha
Brāhmaṇa*, 1, 3, 4, 6.

158,11   *Ṛgveda*, 6, 16, 35.

159,1 *Śatapatha Brāhmaṇa*, 1, 3, 5, 14.

159,19 *Ibid.*, 1, 3, 5, 16.

161,4 *Chāndogya Upaniṣad*, 1, 1, 8.

161,12 J.A.B. van Buitenen, *Akṣara*, cit., p. 180.

161,25 *Bṛhadāraṇyaka Upaniṣad*, 5, 14, 7.

162,1 *Ibid.*, 4, 3, 33.

162,2 *Ṛgveda*, 1, 164, 38.

162,3 *Ibid.*, 3, 60, 3.

162,8 *Ibid.*, 1, 110, 4.

162,19 *Ibid.*, 4, 36, 2.

162,24 *Ibid.*, 10, 80, 7.

162,26 *Ibid.*, 10, 176, 1.

163,7 *Ibid.*, 3, 60, 2.

163,8 S. Kramrisch, "Two," in *Indological Studies in Honor of W. Norman Brown*, American Oriental Society, New Haven, 1962, p. 128.

163,12 *Ṛgveda*, 1, 111, 8.

163,13 *Ibid.*, 4, 33, 3.

164,6 *Ṛgveda*, 1, 110, 2.

164,24 *Ibid.*, 1, 110, 4.

164,26 L. Silburn, *Instant et cause*, de Boccard, Paris, 1989, p. 27.

165,1 *Ṛgveda*, 4, 33, 6.

165,2 *Ibid.*, 1, 161, 5.

165,7 *Loc. cit.*

166,3 *Ibid.*, 1, 161, 1.

166,10 *Aitareya Brāhmaṇa*, 3, 30, 3.

166,16 *Ibid.*, 3, 30, 4.

VIII

169,5 C. G. Jung, "Commentary on 'The Secret of the Golden Flower,'" in *Alchemical Studies*, ed. R.F.C. Hull, in *Collected Works*, Routledge and Kegan Paul, London, vol. XIII, 1978, p. 37.

170,3 Salustius, *On the Gods and the World*, 3, 3.

174,11 M. Blanchot, *Le Livre à venir*, Gallimard, Paris, 1959, p. 242.

174,16 *Ibid.*, p. 243.

176,11 A. E. Housman, "The Name and Nature of Poetry," in *Selected Prose*, ed. J. Carter, Cambridge University Press, Cambridge, 1961, p. 193.

176,14 *Bhagavad Gītā*, 18, 74.

176,23 Th. Gautier, *Souvenirs romantiques*, Garnier, Paris, 1929, p. 267.

176,26 A. K. Coomaraswamy, "Saṃvega: Aesthetic Shock," in *Selected*

	Papers, ed. R. Lipsey,	185,13	*Ibid.*, p. 382.
	Princeton University	185,17	*Ibid.*, p. 381.
	Press, Princeton, N.J.,	185,21	*Ibid.*, p. 380.
	1977, vol. I, p. 179.	185,23	*Ibid.*, p. 381.
180,8	Novalis, "Monolog,"	186,12	*Ibid.*, pp. 381–382.
	in *Schriften*, vol. II,	187,16	M. Proust, ["La
	Kohlhammer,		Poésie ou les lois
	Stuttgart, 1981,		mystérieuses"], in
	pp. 672–673.		*Contre Sainte-Beuve*,
180,23	M. Heidegger,		ed. P. Clarac and
	Unterwegs zur		Y. Sandre,
	Sprache, Neske,		Gallimard, Paris,
	Pfullingen, 1959, p.		1971, p. 417.
	265.	187,17	*Loc. cit.*
182,23	G. Benn, *Briefe*,	188,7	*Ibid.*, p. 418.
	Limes, Wiesbaden,	189,20	*Ibid.*, pp. 419–420.
	1957, pp. 203–204.	191,7	M. Proust, ["Le
184,28	F. Nietzsche, "Über		Déclin de
	Wahrheit und Lüge		l'inspiration"], in
	im aussermoralischen		*Contre Sainte-Beuve*,
	Sinne," in *Werke*, cit.,		cit., p. 423.
	vol. III/2, 1972,	191,11	F. Hölderlin, "Brot
	p. 369.		und Wein," v. 124.
185,6	*Ibid.*, p. 370.	193,7	Pindar, fr. 133,1
185,11	*Ibid.*, p. 374.		(Snell).

A word of thanks to
Claudio Rugafiori,
whose help was precious.

Index